JESUS AND MUHAMMAD

عليهما الصلاة والسلام

Commonalities of Two Great Religions

Daniel Hummel

TUGHRA
BOOKS

New Jersey

Published by Tughra Books
345 Clifton Ave., Clifton,
NJ, 07011, USA

www.tughrabooks.com

Library of Congress Cataloging-in-Publication Data

Names: Hummel, Daniel, author.
Title: Jesus and Muhammad : commonalities of two great religions / Daniel
  Hummel.
Description: First, English edition. | Clifton, New Jersey : Tughra Books,
  2017. | Includes bibliographical references and index.
Identifiers: LCCN 2016020943 | ISBN 9781597849302 (pbk.)
Subjects: LCSH: Islam--Relations--Christianity. | Christianity and other
  religions--Islam. | Muḥammad, Prophet, -632. | Jesus Christ.
Classification: LCC BP172 .H77 2017 | DDC 297.2/83--dc23
LC record available at https://lccn.loc.gov/2016020943

Printed by Marquis in Canada

JESUS AND MUHAMMAD

عليهما الصلاة والسلام

Commonalities of Two Great Religions

Contents

Acknowledgments

This book would not have happened if I did not have the encouragement and support of my loving wife, Dini Hamid Dasuki. After 10 years of marriage and talking about this book through half of it I can finally say that it is officially finished. My beautiful son, Hamza, was also a great inspiration since I wanted him to be proud of me long after I am dead and he can still read this book. I also would like to thank the imams, priests and pastors that I have spoken with throughout the years that helped me to solidify my approach to this book. The good people of this world constantly remind me that the darkness is never permanent and that every person has that spark of goodness within them. I would also like to thank my parents for being supportive. Above all, I would like to thank God because He has been so patient with all my faults. I can only hope that I check out of this world in His good favor.

Perspective

Any book on this subject is bound to have bias. Instead of making the reader guess which perspective the author has on this subject I figured it would be better to be candid. I am an observant Muslim who subscribes to the belief that there is One God who delivered one message to all the Prophets in different times, places and contexts. I believe Jesus is one of the Prophets and only a man.

That being said, I understand that Christians do believe that Jesus is the Son of God. Throughout history Christians have been divided over who Jesus really was up until the present day, so this book is just another perspective within that context. This book will strive for sensitivity while also providing the Muslim perspective which is rarely represented in the literature on this topic. After all Muslims are required to be respectful of all Prophets of which Jesus is considered one of the greatest Prophets in Islam.

I have a vested interest in bridging the divide between Muslims and Christians that currently exists in the world. I am a convert to Islam. My family is mostly Christian with varying levels of faithfulness. They are scattered across the sectarian rainbow from Methodist to Catholic. I was initially raised a Catholic although I spent most of my church time in our local Church of God where I learned a literal Protestant interpretation of the Bible which was actually very helpful in me choosing Islam as my religion.

In my first year of college I began taking an interest in what the Afghans were up to as I was reading stories at the time about the rise of the Taliban. There was one story in the *New York Times* about the efforts of the Taliban to destroy the Buddhist statues in Bamiyan

Province.[1] I was so confused. What was the purpose of dedicating so much effort to destroying those statues? When I learned it had to do with idolatry I was deeply interested in the religion that they were professing that caused them to want to destroy those statues. There was no education about Islam or Islamic culture in public schools when I grew up. Even today, education on Islam or Islamic culture is a higly contentious issue in public schools in America. For example, in Tennnessee recently there has been controversy over teaching about Islam.[2]

It was not long after this that the terrorist attacks of September 11, 2001 occurred which thrust Islam into the spotlight. At some point Islam was talked about by everyone just about everywhere, mostly in a negative light. I began reading a book at this time written by Houston Smith called, *The Illustrated World's Religions: A Guide to Our Wisdom Traditions* for a class on religion.[3] I loved it especially the chapter on Islam. After more research on Islam, I was sold, and in February 2002 I converted to Islam at the Masjid al-Khair (The Good Mosque) in Youngstown, Ohio, which was the closest mosque to me in Western Pennsylvania.

The reaction from my family and friends was confusion. How could you like a religion as violent as Islam? How could you like a religion that oppresses women? How could you choose Muhammad over Jesus? I told my fitness trainer that I converted to Islam who immediately informed me that he was Jewish and would not train me anymore. As a new Muslim I did not have answers to questions about various issues people had with Islam. It also did not help that this was a

---

[1]   Bearak, B. (2001, March 4). "Over World Protests, Taliban Are Destroying Ancient Buddhas." *New York Times* [New York]. Retrieved from www.nytimes. com/2001/03/04/world/over-world-protests-taliban-are-destroying-ancient-buddhas.html

[2]   Blumberg, A. (2016, September 27). Students May Soon Learn Even Less About Islam In Tennessee Public Schools | The Huffington Post. Retrieved from http://www.huffingtonpost.com/entry/students-may-soon-learn-even-less-about-islam-in-tennessee-public-schools_us_57eaa3dae4b0c2407cd9cdb7

[3]   Smith, H. (1995). *The Illustrated World's Religions: A Guide to Our Wisdom Traditions* (1st ed.). San Francisco, CA: HarperOne.

post-9/11 world, but I highly doubt the reactions would have been different. At the same time demagogues of various stripes emerged to profit off of the anti-Muslim fervor including ex-Muslims who wanted to play off the international conflict as an ancient religious rivalry between Christianity and Islam and of course and because they were ex-Muslims, they were considered experts on Islam when that was most often not the case.

Fast forward 12 years later I am much more informed about Islam and the world's religions and how they differ and how they correlate. It has only built my faith in Islam. When I told a colleague that I was writing a book comparing the messages of Jesus and Muhammad she got so upset that I would even attempt to do this. How could you compare them? I realized then that this book needed to be written so that I could rationalize this divide while at the same time provide an even-handed response to this general belief. The diatribes against the Prophet Muhammad are getting more extreme with few recognized responses and an increasing legitimacy given to these comments, which is frightening.

Terms

There are several terms used in this book. The name of the Prophet Muhammad is usually accompanied by the phrase (peace and blessings be upon him) in Islam. This is required for Muslims. It is a bit distracting especially in a book that focuses on the Prophets in which this phrase is supposed to be used for all Prophets. In lull of using this term repeatedly it will be used in absentia in which the reader if s/he is a Muslim could use the term without it being explicitly placed in the text. There are other terms that are used in this book that are listed below in alphabetical order. They will be italicized in the text.

List of Terms

Ahl Al-Kitab –

In English this means 'People of the Book.' This is the Islamic designation for Christians and Jews.

Al-Alim –

This is one of the Names of God in Islam. In English this means 'The All-Knowing.'

Al-Amin –

This is one of the nicknames of the Prophet Muhammad. In English this means 'The Trustworthy.'

Al-Ruh –

In English this means 'The Spirit.' In Islam this is a reference to the Archangel Gabriel who delivered God's messages to His Prophets.

Amana –

This means 'Trust' which is associated in Islam with the Trust of God given to mankind to maintain His creation and follow His commands. This is also used in contracts to indicate a Trust between investors and fund managers, for example.

Al-Sadiq/Siddiq –

In English this means 'The Truthful One' or 'The One who Bears Witness to the Truth.' This was a title given to Abu Bakr after the Night Journey of the Prophet Muhammad when many rejected his claims to have made the journey to Jerusalem and to Heaven in one night. Abu Bakr confirmed the account of Muhammad earning him this title.

Bani –

In English this means 'Tribe.'

Bid'a –

In English this means 'Innovation.' This term is used in Islam to indicate innovation in religion which is strictly prohibited.

Caliph –

A Caliph in Islam is a leader of the Muslim state. There were 4 Rightly-Guided Caliphs in Islam who were Abu Bakr, Umar, Uthman and Ali, in that order. Afterwards, the Caliph rotated between competing Islamic empires until it was dissolved in the early 20th century after the collapse of the Ottoman Empire.

Da'if –

In English this means 'Weak.' It is a term given to the attributed traditions of the Prophet Muhammad that have been deemed inauthentic according to the discipline of hadith.

Dajjal –

This is one of the entities that will appear at the end times according to Islam. Its closest counterpart in Christianity would be the Anti-Christ.

Dhikr –

In English this is 'remembrance.' In particular in Islam this refers to the regular remembrance of God.

Hadith –

A tradition in Islam that reports the words, deeds and approvals of the Prophet Muhammad or one of his companions. In short, the way he lived his life. This is the second source for Islamic beliefs after the Qur'an.

Hadith Qudsi –

This is a type of hadith called a sacred report. It is a narration, which from the perspective of its meaning, is from God and, which from the perspective of its wording, is from the Prophet Muhammad.

Halal –

In English it means 'permissible or lawful.' Halal is the status given to anything that is permissible in Islam.

Hijra –

In English it means 'Migration.' There were two major migrations in early Islamic history. There was the migration of some Muslims to Ethiopia while the Prophet Muhammad was still in Mecca and there was the major migration of most Muslims to Medina including the Prophet. This second migration marks the beginning of the Hijri (lunar) calendar used in Islam.

Hudud –

In English it means 'Capital Punishments.' These punishments represent a subset of Islamic Law (Sharia).

Ikhlas –

In English this means 'sincerity or piety.' In Islam sincerity is needed in all actions in that this sincerity is directed towards the pleasure of God alone.

Isnad –

In English this means 'chain.' It is a concept known in the discipline of hadith in which the chain of narrators are recorded in the reporting of a hadith to determine its authenticity. There are entire books written on these hadith narrators.

Jinn –

This is an invisible entity that was made of fire. This creation of God also has the ability to choose between right and wrong. The Devil is one of these creatures.

Ka'ba –

This is the building at the center of the Masjid al-Haram complex in Mecca. Muslims perform a pilgrimage here once in their lifetime if they have the means. Muslims all over the world pray in the direction of this building.

Mahdi –

This is one of the entities that will appear at the end of time according to Islam. This person or group will unite the Muslims against their enemies and renew vigor in the religion of Islam. Most of what is known about the Mahdi is contained in the hadith literature.

Masjid al-Aqsa –

This is the mosque located in Jerusalem and the third holiest site in Islam. It was the original direction for prayer for the Muslims until the direction was changed in Medina towards Mecca.

Mu'ahid –

This is a designation for a peaceful non-Muslim. A peaceful non-Muslim is one that is not in a fight with the Muslims or trying to take their land or prevent the spread of Islam. He has an agreement with the Muslims. It is forbidden in Islam to harm this person.

Nasikh –

In English this is 'abrogation.' This concept covers the topic of Qur'anic abrogation when one verse replaces another earlier verse.

Qadi –

In English this is 'judge.' The judge in Islam is central to both criminal and civil proceedings that require interpretations of Islamic Law (*sharia*).

Qira'at –

This is a recitation of the Qur'an. There are 10 variant accepted readings of the Qur'anic text.

Qisas –

This is part of the *hudud* (capital punishments) in Islamic Law. It is reciprocal punishment in which murder is reciprocated by death to the perpetrator unless blood money is accepted in exchange for the capital punishment.

Ramadan –

One of the months in the Islamic calendar. This is the holiest month of the calendar in which the Qur'an was first revealed. Muslims fast from dawn to dusk during this month.

Sahih –

In English this is 'authentic.' In the discipline of hadith this is the status given to a hadith when it has been determined to be authentic.

Salamun Alaikum / As-Salamu Alaykum –

In English this is 'Peace be Upon you.' It is the Islamic greeting.

Sharia–

Islamic law derived from the text of the Qur'an, the traditions of the Prophet Muhammad and the work of Muslim scholars throughout the centuries.

Sirah –

This is one of the genre in the Islamic literature. It is the story of the life of the Prophet Muhammad and the events that occurred during his lifetime.

Sujud –

In English this is 'prostration.' In Islamic prayer the face is placed on the floor.

Tafsir –

In English this is 'exegesis or interpretation.' There are various interpretations of the verses of the Qur'an with several official interpretations that are widely accepted in the Muslim world by learned scholars in Islam.

Taqiyyah –

In general, it is a concept in Islam that allows the Muslim to deny his/her faith in times of personal danger. It has multiple meanings.

Taqwa –

In English this is 'fear of God' / 'being mindful of God' / 'being God-conscious.'

Ummah –

A term in Islam that implies a community which can be both broad and the narrow in its application. In today's usage it is a term used to consolidate all Muslims in the world in one singular 'brotherhood.'

Yawm –

In English this is 'period.' It is used in the Qur'an to refer to phases which is sometimes translated as days.

List of Qur'anic Chapters

Meccan Chapters in a Modified al-Zarkashi Order

The First Three Years

96: al-Alaq: The Clot
73: al-Muzzammil: The Enshrouded One
74: al-Muddaththir: The Cloaked One
81: al-Takwir: The Overthrowing
87: al-Ala: The Most High
92: al-Layl: The Night
93: al-Duha: The Morning Hours
94: al-Inshirah: Solace
103: al-Asr: The Declining Day
100: al-Adiyat: The Chargers
102: al-Takathur: The Competition
107: al-Ma'un: The Small Kindnesses
112: al-Ikhlas: Sincerity
97: al-Qadr: Night of Power / Fate
95: al-Tin: The Fig
101: al-Qaria: The Calamity
75: al-Qiyama: The Resurrection
104: al-Humaza: The Gossip-Monger

Later Meccan Chapters

68: al-Qalam: The Pen
111: al-Masad: The Flame
89: al-Fajr: The Dawn

108: al-Kawthar: Abundance

109: al-Kafirun: The Disbelievers

53: al-Najm: The Star

80: Abasa: He Frowned

91: al-Shams: The Sun

85: al-Buruj: Constellations

77: al-Mursalat: The Emissaries

50: Qaf

90: al-Balad: The City

86: al-Tariq: The Morning Star

54: al-Qamar: The Moon

38: Sad: The Letter Sad

7: al-Araf: The Heights

69: al-Haaqqa: The Reality

72: al-Jinn

36: Ya-Sin

25: al-Furqan: The Criterion

35: Fatir: The Angels

19: Maryam: Mary

20: Ta-Ha

56: al-Waqia: The Event

26: al-Shuara: The Poets

27: al-Naml: The Ants

28: Qasas: The Narrations

17: al-Isra: The Night Journey

10: Yunus: Jonah

11: Hud

12: Yusuf: Joseph

15: al-Hijr: The Rocky Tract

6: al-An'am: The Cattle

37: al-Saffat: Those Who Set the Ranks

31: Luqman

34: Saba

39: al-Zumar: The Troops

40: al-Mumin: The Believer

41: Fussilat: Explained in Detail

42: al-Shura: The Council

43: al-Zukhruf: Ornaments of Gold

44: al-Dukhan: The Smoke

45: al-Jathiya: Crouching

46: al-Ahqaf: The Wind-Curved Sandhills

51: al-Dhariyat: The Winnowing Winds

88: al-Ghashiya: The Overwhelming

18: al-Kahf: The Cave

16: al-Nahl: The Bee

71: Nuh: Noah

14: Ibrahim: Abraham

21: al-Anbiya: The Prophets

23: al-Mu'minun: The Believers

32: al-Sajda: The Prostration

52: al-Tur: The Mount

67: al-Mulk: The Sovereignty

70: al-Maarij: The Ascending Stairways

78: al-Naba: The Tidings

79: al-Naziat: Soul Snatchers

82: al-Infitaar: The Cleaving

84: al-Inshiqaq: The Sundering

Chapters Added by Numan b. Bashir

30: al-Rum: The Byzantines

29: al-Ankabut: The Spider

83: al-Mutaffifin: The Cheaters

Meccan Chapters Excluded from This Book

105: al-Fil: The Elephant

113: al-Falaq: The Daybreak

114: al-Nas: Mankind

106: Quraysh

Medinan Chapters Used in this Book

2: al-Baqarah: The Cow

8: al-Anfal: The Spoils of War

3: Al Imran: The Family of Imran

33: al-Ahzab: The Coalition

60: al-Mumtahanah: She that is examined

4: al-Nisaa: The Women

65: al-Talaq: The Divorce

22: al-Hajj: The Pilgrimage

9: al-Tawba: The Repentance

5: al-Maida: The Table

Prologue

This book has been in development for more than five years. At first it was inspired by the multitude of publications and online rhetoric that has increased in recent years on the "stark" differences that exist between Jesus conceptualized as the Son of God in Christianity and the Prophet Muhammad conceptualized as the Final Messenger in Islam. The publications and online rhetoric have mostly come from Christians although not representative of Christian opinion everywhere.

Muslims revere Jesus as a Prophet of God. Insulting or hurting the name of Jesus is a sin much like it is when doing the same with the name of Muhammad. The vitriol of these comparisons between Jesus and Muhammad cast Muhammad as the most evil man to ever have lived possibly in a desperate attempt to drive a wedge between Christians and Muslims. Encouragingly, there also exists a lot of work that attempt to remove this wedge by finding commonalities between Christianity and Islam.

A pure comparison of the careers of Jesus and Muhammad is seemingly impossible. Jesus was raised amongst the monotheist followers of Moses. Muhammad was raised amongst the polytheist Arabs who had contact with monotheist peoples, but did not embrace their religion. Jesus preached for a short time while Muhammad preached for a much longer time. Jesus did not have at his command an army nor did he have enough standing in his community to be a leader while Muhammad had both. Jesus mostly moved from town to town while Muhammad stayed in Mecca and eventually Medina. There was an attempt to kill Jesus while Muhammad died of an illness despite the many attempts to kill him.

These differences in situations although not comprehensive indicate the challenge in comparing these two men. Logically one can conclude that given different circumstances the messages of the two men from God would necessarily be different. This work does not gloss over these differences. Instead, concepts are considered as broadly as possible while contexts are narrowed as best as possible to match their careers. This is not done in other work on these two great men. Instead, they are compared flatly leading readers to believe Muhammad was a war-monger while Jesus was a peace-loving and sacrificial man. This approach is blatantly rejected in this book.

For example, how can one compare one president to another in the history of the United States without taking into consideration the events that occurred during their presidencies? If one is evaluating a presidency based on whether it was good or bad following subjective criteria than the main goal is determining how s/he reacted to certain events and the outcome of that action. Whether one is Christian or Muslim the goal of Jesus and Muhammad was to establish God's Will on Earth and further faith in Him alone. The ultimate objective was to save souls. The purpose of life was/is to serve God and through faith in God serve man. Can one say that those missions have been successful? Certainly together Christianity and Islam compose about half the world's population. There is no doubt that long after everyone on the planet is dead and mostly forgotten these two men, Jesus and Muhammad, will be remembered by everyone until the end of time.

The point is that although this is a comparison of Jesus and Muhammad, the comparison is not like comparing presidents. One can easily ascribe the success of Islam to warfare and Christianity to the winning of hearts through love and service, but is that true? Based on existential realities Jesus and Muhammad are both equally successful in saving souls (winning converts) and establishing God's Will on Earth despite the ups and downs of history. This comparison does not consider the outcomes, but the teachings confined by the realities of the time and place. In this regard, this book is a valued contribution to the ongoing dialogues between Muslims and Christians on their respective leaders.

CHAPTER 1

INTRODUCTION

Introduction

The contexts of Muhammad and Jesus were different. Is it possible to narrow those contexts so that they are as similar as possible so those teachings can be compared? Fortunately, they are. Muhammad had several major periods in his life that can be clearly separated from the whole. The first period used in this book is the first three years after the first revelation. This period is clearly separated by the command to begin preaching Islam publicly which can be found in Chapter 15[4] verses 94 to 97.[5] Before Islam was preached publicly it was maintained in secret. Although it is not known accurately for how long Jesus preached, many consider his preaching to have lasted for three years which is the perspective from the Gospel of John. The other gospels shorten his preaching to a much shorter time period such as a year or less.[6] This time period allows a time element consistency between the initial teachings of Muhammad and the teachings of Jesus.

Another contextual factor is conditions. Jesus preached with a minimal following of disciples before his departure. Muhammad also preached with a minimal number of followers until his migration from Mecca to Medina. During this time period Muhammad was embattled, mocked and undermined without a strong base of support or sizable number of followers. The conditional circumstances of Jesus during his preaching were the same. Given these similarities the entire Mec-

---

4   The names of these chapters in chronological order can be found in the section 'List of Qur'anic Chapters' on pp. 19-22 above.

5   Quran Tafsir Ibn Kathir - Home. (2010, March). Retrieved from www.qtafsir.com.

6   Ehrman, B. D. (2009). *Jesus, interrupted: Revealing the hidden contradictions in the Bible (and why we don't know about them)*. New York, NY: HarperOne.

can period of revelation of the Qur'an serves as a point of comparison between the teachings of Jesus and Muhammad.

Unfortunately, there are some contexts that cannot be controlled, such as differences in the people. The Jewish tribes had the Torah which Jesus affirmed amongst them (Matthew 5:17). The Arab tribes did not have this and were mostly polytheists. The time in history was different, and so were political and economic dynamics. There were also different languages and idiomatic expressions. These differences in context cannot be controlled, but can only be mentioned.

In essence, this is the main focus of this book. Jesus preached in similar circumstances to Muhammad while Muhammad was still in Mecca. If another city would have offered Jesus a refuge similar to Muhammad with control of its affairs than a perfect comparison in teachings would be made on their entire lives. Would Jesus have marched in armies of believers as Muhammad did? Certainly Moses and the Prophets of Israel did before Jesus, and Jesus never denounced those Prophets. What about the other teachings on state and society that were revealed in Medina by Muhammad?

The goal of this book is to compare these two great men and determine how similar or different their teachings are to each other. Similarities raise interesting points of contact between Christianity and Islam. A believing Muslim would attribute these similarities to the One God who sent Prophets/Messengers with the same inalienable message. A believing Christian might attribute these similarities to mere coincidence or to Muhammad plagiarizing the teachings of Jesus. This claim was even made at the time of the Prophet Muhammad (16:103; 44:14). An atheist would probably make a similar claim about all Prophets including Jesus in which he simply added to what was already being taught from the Prophets of old times.

Differences and contradictions are also interesting because in essence this has been what most books and internet tirades have been about regarding these men. Again, the believing Muslim would attribute such differences to devious scribes and the inconsistencies of transmission of biblical knowledge as well as problems with translation. Biblical scholarship has confirmed these possibilities.[7] The believing Christian may find these differences to be proof that it is not the same message therefore Muhammad is a fake. The arguments are usually a double-edged sword.

There are also items found in one message that may not be found in the other. These messages also present a challenge to the harmony of these teachings and provoke similar responses from believing Muslims and Christians when there are differences and contradictions. There are also some teachings of Jesus that cannot be found in the Meccan period of Islam, but can be found in the Medinan period.

The book is organized around the teachings of these two men. The teachings of Muhammad stand as the organizing teachings for the book mostly because there are more of them than the Gospel produces. The Qur'an serves as the primary source of the teachings of Muhammad while the four books of the Gospel in the Bible serve as the primary source of the teachings of Jesus. The *hadith* and epistles of Paul as well as other miscellaneous books of the New Testament are not included in this book unless to help clarify a point. The translation of the Qur'an by Abdullah Yusuf Ali[8] was used while both the New American Version of the Catholic Bible[9] and the New International Version of the Protestant Bible[10] were used for this book.

In addition to the Qur'an, there are two other sources available in Islam which help to understand the verses and the context in which those verses were revealed. The first source is the *tafsir* of Ibn Kathir which is one of the most authoritative commentaries on the Qur'an in the Muslim world. The *tafsir* of Ibn Kathir is considered to be more conservative than others. The use of this *tafsir* also indicates that even with a more conservative approach the interpretations discussed here

---

7   Ehrman, B. D. (2007). *Misquoting Jesus: The story behind who changed the Bible and why*. New York, NY: HarperSanFrancisco.

8   Ali, A. Y. (2010). *The Meaning of the Glorious Qur'an*. Istanbul, Turkey: ASIR Media.

9   International Bible Society. (1984). The Bible: New International Version. Colorado Springs, CO: International Bible Society.

10 American Bible Society. (2002). New American Bible: Including the revised Psalms and the Revised New Testament. New York: American Bible Society.

can be found in the Qur'an. This *tafsir* was first published in 1370 AD after his death and was translated into English in 2000. The website qtafsir.com was used for the source of this *Tafsir*.[11] The second source is the *sirah* of Ibn Ishaq[12] and Martin Lings[13] which are two sources for the life and times of the Prophet Muhammad.[14]

This book is mostly descriptive with pockets of analysis that can be found at the end of each chapter and in chapters 10, 11 and 14. Chapters 10 and 11 are mostly interpretive analyses on the differences and similarities between the teachings in the Gospels and the Qur'an. Chapter 14 is a general summary of the book. The reason that a descriptive approach was taken is because the desire was to not only uncover these similarities and differences, but to be a source for this comparison. There is no question that Muslims and Christians reading this book will want to explore these verses on their own through their own interpretive lens. They may disagree with my interpretations at the end of each chapter, but at the very least they have a clear proof of the location of these verses and a brief description to accompany them.

The second chapter of this book is specifically on the first three years of the mission of the Prophet Muhammad and the teachings in these years. These accounts utilize recognized life stories of Muhammad as well as recognized scholars' determination of what Qur'anic revelations are within the first three years. Verses from the Qur'an are separated by theme and are extracted due to uniqueness and substance.

The third chapter of this book matches the teachings of Jesus in his ministry that coincide with the teachings in Islam during the first three years of the mission of Muhammad. The teachings that contradict the teachings in Islam or cannot be found in Islam are discussed in a later

---

[11]   Quran Tafsir Ibn Kathir - Home. (2010, March). Retrieved from www.qtafsir.com/.

[12]   Guillaume, A. (2002). *The Life of Muhammad* (M. Al-Saqqa, I. Al-Abyari, & A.H. Shalabi). New York, NY: Oxford Uni. Press. (Original work published 1937).

[13]   Lings, M. (2006). *Muhammad: His life based on the earliest sources* (2nd ed.). Rochester, VT: Inner Traditions Publishers.

[14]   These sources including the holy books will not be cited every time they are used throughout the book unless a direct quote is taken from them or it is necessary to indicate where the information is coming from and it is not clear in the text.

chapter of the book. These teachings are isolated to similarities in context and in time which provide the best point for comparison between the two men.

Chapters four to nine of this book focus on the last ten years in Mecca during the ministry of the Prophet Muhammad. New themes are elaborated on using the same methodology as that used to extract verses in the second chapter. The teachings of Jesus that coincide with these teachings are compared to the teachings of Muhammad during this final period in Mecca. Unlike chapter 2, the teachings of Muhammad and the teachings of Jesus are part of a single chapter due to the large number of themes that emerge in this last period of Islam in Mecca during the time of Muhammad.

The tenth chapter of this book addresses teachings that conflict between Jesus and Muhammad. There are not many of these verses but most of them are contained in either the Gospel of Matthew or the Gospel of John. The possible reasons for the divergences are considered including contextual differences and problems with transmission / translation.

The eleventh chapter explores further similarities between the teachings of Jesus and Muhammad which include revelations from the Medinan era. The first chapters of this book attempt to narrow the context and time period for the preaching of their messages, but this chapter utilizes the teachings of Jesus that resonate in the Qur'an not only during the Meccan period. This neglect in context and time period is common in comparisons between Jesus and Muhammad. The point of this chapter is to show that although some of the teachings of Jesus did not appear in the Meccan period, they did appear in the Medinan era.

The twelfth chapter considers some of the verses in the Gospel of John that refer to the coming of another 'entity' that will complete the religion of the followers of Jesus. Muslims have long interpreted these verses as direct references to the Prophet Muhammad. This conceptualization is explored in this chapter.

The thirteenth chapter is a refutation to common accusations made about Islam. This chapter addresses some of the points commonly raised such as the relationship between Islam and violence and the opression of women. Other points are also discussed, however the chapter only addresses some of the major issues and is not comprehensive.

The fourteenth chapter draws together the chapter summaries. One of the major recommendations made in this chapter is the need for Muslims and Christians to work harder in seeing the commonalities in their faith for further cooperation instead of continual conflict. In this regard, this conclusion clearly separates this book from other books on these two great men which aim to create deeper divisions.

Chapter 2

THE FIRST THREE YEARS

The First Three Years

The Meccan chapters of the Qur'an were separated from the Medinan chapters through the scholarship of Imam Muhammad al-Zarkashi, who was from Egypt and lived and died around the time of Ibn Kathir in the 14th century AD. His listing of the chapters of the Qur'an in order from first revelation to the final revelation and between Meccan and Medinan is widely accepted across the Muslim world as accurate. Another listing was developed by Nu'man b. Bashir which is much older than the list developed by al-Zarkashi. He was born in Medina not long after the migration of the Prophet Muhammad from Mecca to Medina. He was a governor of Kufa and a judge in Damascus. His ordering follows al-Zarkashi, except he includes chapters 30, 29 and 83 as Meccan chapters. There is some debate about the inclusion of these chapters as Meccan chapters, especially chapters 29 and 83. These are all included along with the listing by al-Zarkashi as Meccan chapters. This ordering is used in this book to separate out the Meccan chapters as well as those early chapters that were included in the first three years of the Prophet Muhammad's mission.[15]

The first three years of the mission of the Prophet Muhammad is marked by the period when the messages of Islam were communicated in private before the command from God that they be proclaimed in public. The verses that end the period of private communication of the revelations are Chapter 15 verses 94 through 97. Before these verses, the themes of the verses in the first three years included the importance of prayer, the importance of proper ablution (washing

---

15   Von Denffer, A. (2009). Ulum al Qur'an: An introduction to the sciences of the Qur'an (2nd ed.). Leicestershire, UK: The Islamic Foundation Publishers.

for prayer), recognition of God as al-Rahman (the Most Merciful), reassurances to the Prophet Muhammad of his Prophethood, the ephemeral nature of earthly things, death and resurrection, hell and paradise, the glory of God, the Oneness of God, patience in adversity, the Islamic greeting of peace and other Islamic colloquialisms and the marvels of nature.[16]

These themes, the *sirah* of Muhammad, and the pre-persecution of the Muslims serve as a means to determine which chapters were revealed in this initial period of Islam. The *sirah* of Muhammad contains the stories behind the chapters while the lack of persecution of the Muslims during this period conditioned those early chapters to focus on issues other than the persecution, which became one of the focuses after this period. The *sirah* literature is one of the most important elements in establishing these chapters in the first three years of the mission of Islam. Ibn Ishaq's *Sîratu Rasûl Allâh* is probably the most comprehensive that exists despite the problems that many Islamic scholars have had with the work.[17] Martin Lings' *Muhammad: His Life Based on the Earliest Sources* is also considered an authoritative account of the life of Muhammad.[18] These two *sirahs* are used in this book.

There were some challenges in using al-Zarkashi's order and relying on the themes of the first three years of the Qur'an. There were some early chapters in the order that had themes that clearly indicated that the chapter came after the first three years of revelation. Usually these were references to the persecution of the Muslims, etc. After Chapter 100 the chapters became difficult to clearly separate between these two periods. Based on the methodology employed in this book some reworking of the order developed by al-Zarkashi was relied on to clearly separate those chapters revealed in the first three years from the other chapters. In this case, Chapters 68, 111 and 89 were considered

---

[16] Lings, M. (2006). *Muhammad: His life based on the earliest sources* (2nd ed.). Rochester, VT: Inner Traditions Publishers.

[17] Guillaume, A. (2002). *The Life of Muhammad* (M. Al-Saqqa, I. Al-Abyari, & A.H. Shalabi). New York, NY: Oxford Uni. Press. (Original work published 1937).

[18] Lings, 2006, op.cit.

later Meccan chapters while Chapters 102, 107, 112, 97, 95, 101, 75, and 104 were considered early Meccan chapters. In addition, Chapters 108, 109, 53, 80, 91, 85, and 77 were considered later Meccan chapters. The general order of these chapters was maintained, but as a group they were categorized as either early or later Meccan chapters. Lastly, four chapters were difficult to categorize at the theme level. These were Chapters 105, 113, 114, and 106. This listing of these chapters in this order which is referred to as a modified al-Zarkashi order with titles is in the section 'List of Qur'anic Chapters' on pages 19 to 22 in this book.

According to the two sources used to separate these chapters, Muhammad had been experiencing visions before his first revelations. He sought retreat in Mt. Hira outside Mecca. This is where he experienced his first revelation which is the famous first five verses of Chapter 96. During this first revelation the angel Gabriel continued to squeeze Muhammad insisting that he read, which was confusing to him because he was unlettered. The main point of this chapter is that God has exalted man by giving him knowledge.[19]

After this encounter he ran to his wife Khadijah worried that he may be possessed. She reassured him while covering him that due to his good behaviors nothing bad was happening. She consulted with her cousin Waraqah b. Nawfal, a Christian, who reassured her that he was a Messenger of God.[20]

Following this initial revelation, another revelation did not come for a while which caused Muhammad to despair greatly. Eventually Chapters 73 and 74 were revealed. Chapter 73 enjoined the Prophet to stand in prayer at night in which each verse was to be recited slowly with elongated letters with pauses between verses. Chapter 74 bestowed Messengership on Muhammad. In this chapter issues of purity, Oneness and Unity of God and selflessness are covered. Purity is referring to clothes and intentions. The Oneness of God is a direct refutation of idols that were popular at the time of Muhammad. Self-

---

[19] Guillaume, 2002, op.cit.

[20] Lings, 2006, op.cit.

lessness is referring to the giving of gifts without return and being patient in that giving.[21]

Initially, Muhammad communicated these revelations only to those closest to him with some followers. The first to believe in him was his wife, Khadijah. Ali believed in him next followed by Zayd, the freed slave of Muhammad, and then Abu Bakr. These revelations made no demands on these followers initially, but these early followers followed the commands given to the Prophet in prayer and cleanliness. For instance, the proper way to perform the washing before prayer was taught to Muhammad by Gabriel. Muhammad then showed his wife how to do it.[22]

Muhammad and the early followers sometimes would go out to the glens of Mecca to pray and return at night. These early companions would memorize the revelations of the Qur'an and chant them in prayer. Eventually, a revelation came that commanded the Prophet to preach openly.[23]

Three years had passed while more revelations had come following Chapters 73 and 74. Utilizing the themes distilled by Lings along with the chronological order of the Qur'anic chapters by al-Zarkashi and Nu'man b. Bashir as well as the *sirahs* of both Lings and Ibn Ishaq, several Qur'anic chapters were selected that represent the revelations of the first three years of the Prophet's mission. Each of these chapters is discussed under the general themes of which it belongs in the following sections.

2.1. Importance of Prayer

In Chapter 87 verses 14 to 15 it states that the people who prosper are those that purify themselves and glorify the Name of God in prayer. Ibn Kathir explained that one should purify his negative characteristics and follow the commands of God in which prayer is one of those commands at appointed times. Purification is not just referring to the ablution for prayer, but the purity of the heart as well. Purity was already

---

[21]   Quran Tafsir Ibn Kathir - Home. (2010, March). Retrieved from www.qtafsir.com/.

[22]   Guillaume, 2002, op.cit.

[23]   Ibid.

mentioned in Chapter 74 before this chapter. In this chapter it is expressly linked with prayer. Prayer is one of the tools to purify one's heart. In a way the ritual ablution for prayer taught to the Prophet by Gabriel in this early stage of revelation is a preparation for the greater purity that derives from prayer.

The use of prayer to purify the heart is one of the reasons that it is stated in Chapter 107 verses 4 to 6 that those who pray either to be seen or do so in a mindless way are those who deny Judgment Day as stated in verse 1 in this chapter. Ibn Kathir explained these verses that there are three interpretations possible. These verses could be a direct reference to the hypocrites who pray to be seen which would place these verses and this chapter in the Medinan period when the community of Muslims had many problems with hypocritical Muslims. It could also be a reference to those who are heedless of prayer by waiting to pray at the last minute for the prescribed daily prayers or not fulfilling the conditions of prayer such as not praying it correctly. Lastly, it could be because the person who prays is mindless during his prayer without focusing on it and God. The last of these explanations seems more plausible for the first three years of the Muslim community in Mecca.

The centrality of prayer to these revelations of the Qur'an is further reinforced in Chapter 97. This chapter refers to the night the Qur'an began to be revealed in which worship during this night is equivalent to worship during 1000 months. This night is traditionally unknown exactly, but occurs sometime in the last 10 days of the fasting month of *Ramadan*.[24]

Prayer is emphasized throughout the Qur'an including the rest of the Meccan period. It is mentioned more throughout the remainder of the Meccan period than any of the other themes first established in the first three years of Islam. In Chapter 20 verse 132, prayer should be the first priority in which sustenance for this life should be secondary. Ibn Kathir cited a *hadith* of the Prophet in which he said that if the Hereafter is the intention of the person, then his situation in this life will be made easy for him.

---

24 Qur'an Tafsir, 2010, op.cit.

The importance of prayer can be found in other later Meccan verses such as Chapter 31 verse 17 where Luqman, a wise man, is giving advice to his son. In this verse he advised his son to perform prayer. This activity is listed along with forbidding evil and supporting good and being patient with what happens in this life. This final point is also amongst the themes in the first three years of Islam.

Another later Meccan verse that emphasizes prayer in Islam is Chapter 29 verse 45 where prayer is described as a tool to resist shameful and unjust deeds. Ibn Kathir added more points on prayer in which it has two characteristics. It leads one to give up immoral behavior and evil deeds and is used in remembering God. In this verse the remembrance of God is described as the greatest thing in life. It follows the emphasis on establishing prayer. Further Ibn Kathir delineated true prayer from false prayer. True prayer has three attributes, which are sincerity in purpose (only for God), fear of God, and remembrance of God.

Those people have fear of God or are mindful of God, i.e. who are with *taqwa*. Prayer is also elaborated on in another later group of Meccan verses in Chapter 51 verses 17 to 18. In these verses the people who have *taqwa* are described. They are people who sleep a little at night because they pray at night. The night prayer was enjoined on Muhammad in the initial revelations during the first three years. Ibn Kathir added in his explanation of these verses that in the last 1/3 of the night God is more receptive of repentance and grants/answers prayers.

Finally, in Chapter 32 verse 16, which is a later Meccan verse on prayer, the issue of praying at night is reiterated. Those who do this are again described as having *taqwa*, but also hope for His Mercy. They fear His punishment which is what the fear of God means.

2.2. Reassurances to the Prophet

There are a number of reassurances to Muhammad in the first three years of revelation and beyond. This is rational considering that the initial experience of revelation was traumatic for him and the natural insecurities that all men face when given a weighty mission. God explains in Chapter 81 that the Qur'an is truly from an honorable messenger, i.e. Gabriel, and Muhammad is not possessed and therefore the Qur'an is not from the Devil.

The authenticity of the revelation was a deep concern of the Prophet. He was afraid he would forget it after it was revealed to him. In Chapter 87 verses 6 to 7, God informed the Prophet that He would teach him the revelation so that he would not forget. Further, He assured Muhammad that whatever he forgot it was the Will of God. Muhammad was told again about this in Chapter 75 verses 16 to 19 in which he should just listen while it was being communicated to him by Gabriel.

Another instance of reassurance appears in Chapter 93 which confirmed that Muhammad would receive a great deal in the Hereafter. In verses 4 to 5, God explained to him that the Hereafter would be better than the present and He would give him what pleased him. In Chapter 94 verse 2, according to Ibn Kathir, the removal of the burden from the Prophet was the forgiveness of his sins (past and future).

The reassurances that were given the Prophet in the first three years took a different direction in the last ten years of his period in Mecca. The public preaching of Islam began after the first three years which increased the attacks of the unbelievers on Islam and the Prophet. At this point many of the revelations addressed these attacks. This subject is covered in more detail in Chapter 4 on the issue of disbelief in the later Meccan verses.

2.3. Ephemeral Nature of Worldly Things

In Chapter 87 verses 16 to 17, it is stated that man prefers the life of this world over the life in the next world despite the Hereafter being better. Ibn Kathir provided a saying of the Prophet Muhammad in his explanation of these verses that whoever loves this life will receive it but suffer in the next life and vice versa for those who love the next life. The Hereafter is everlasting while the current life is temporary. The verses and this saying strongly indicate that this world is fleeting and ephemeral.

This theme appears again in Chapter 93 verse 4, which was already discussed above regarding the reassurances to the Prophet. For all people the Hereafter is better than this life so one should work for that. Ibn Kathir solidified this point in his explanation of this verse by using the Prophet as an example. He described him as the most abstinent of the people in worldly things and worldly matters.

The issue of wealth naturally is covered regarding the ephemeral nature of worldly things. The revelations point out that man loves wealth more than anything. In Chapter 100 verse 8 it asserts that man is violent in his love of wealth. In Chapter 104 verses 2 to 3 Ibn Kathir explained these verses that man loves counting his wealth in which he thinks it will cause him to last forever, but the end of this person is the Hellfire.

Chapter 102 adds more to the point of man's obsession with wealth. Ibn Kathir added many comments to this chapter. He included many statements, *hadiths*, of the Prophet. One statement reports that if man had one valley full with gold, he would want another one. Another statement points out that man only gets three benefits from wealth which are what he eats and wears as worldly benefits and that which he donates to charity which adds to his betterment in the Hereafter.

In the later Meccan verses in Chapter 18 verse 7 the world is described as temporary which only has transient beauty. In contrast, life is a test to determine who are the best among the people. This test determines who will enter heaven or not.

2.4. Death, Resurrection and Final Judgment

In Chapter 75 verse 36 God questions if man thinks that he will be left without control or without purpose. The question is posed to man. Ibn Kathir explained that man has received commands and prohibitions from God because man was not neglected or left alone to do as he pleases. Further, as explained by Ibn Kathir, man will not be neglected in the grave and he will be resurrected. The title of this chapter establishes this theme.

There are a number of verses in the first three years of revelation in Islam that describe the scenes and activities of the Day of Judgment. In Chapter 81 a number of signs of the Day of Judgment are described. Some of these events are repeated in Chapter 101.

In these verses the emphasis on good deeds and accountability on the Day of Judgment also appear. In Chapter 81 verse 7 it is stated that the souls will be sorted out on Judgment Day. In Chapter 100 verses 7 and 10 to 11 indicate that what was in peoples' souls will be exposed during this judgment in which each person's deeds will be compensated for with no injustice for anyone. Further, people will be questioned regarding the favors of God upon each person which is shown in Chapter 102 verse 8. Ibn Kathir related a tradition in regards this verse which notes that there are two favors mankind mis-uses which are his/her health and free time. In chapter 101 verses 6 to 9 it states that those good deeds will be measured against bad deeds and whichever dominates will determine the direction for one's eternity. These deeds are recorded on a scroll which is handed to each person on the Day of Judgment in Chapter 81 verse 10 according to Ibn Kathir's explanation.

The accumulation of good deeds in this life is emphasized in Islam in order to achieve a favorable outcome on the Day of Judgment. In Chapter 103 in verses 2 to 3, man is considered in loss except those who have faith and do good deeds. Additionally, Chapter 92 indicates in verses 5 to 10 that the path of evil is made easy for one who thinks himself/herself to be self-sufficient and the path of good is made easy for the one who fears God.

Ibn Kathir commented on the paths of good and evil regarding the concept of pre-destination / fate. Belief in fate is one of the six princi-ples of faith in Islam. Abu Bakr, one of the first companions of the Prophet, asked about this and whether the doing of good deeds had any relevance if everything is pre-decided. The Prophet responded that the good or bad deeds are made easier depending on this pre-deter-mined status, thus the doing of good deeds is not negated for all men/women who seek the Hereafter.

Judgment Day also appears in later Meccan verses and through-out the Qur'an. In Chapter 7 verse 187 the people who ask about the timing of Judgment Day are addressed. The recommended answer in this verse is that only God knows when it will be. Judg-ment Day is also referred to again in Chapter 78 verse 40 in which all the deeds that one has done in his/her life will be presented to him/her. At that time the unbelievers will wish they were dust, i.e. not created, according to the explanation of Ibn Kathir. In addition, in Chapter 77 verses 7 to 10, it is promised that Judgment Day will occur and specifically in verses 8 to 10 a number of events are described to occur during this Day.

2.5. Hell and Paradise

The goal of doing good deeds is to achieve Paradise / Heaven and to avoid Hell. This topic is intimately connected to the previous discussion on death, resurrection and judgment. In Chapter 92 verses 14 to 16, God warns of the blazing fire. This is reinforced by those who will enter it and those who will be far from it. In a later Meccan chapter, Chapter 77 verses 30 to 33 describe Hell in some detail in connection with those who are criminals and will enter it.

It is interesting that these verses follow the verses on pre-destination which were covered in the previous section. Ibn Kathir added his commentary to these verses that no one will enter Hell except those who disobey the Prophet Muhammad. Additionally, the righteous people will not go to Hell according to Ibn Kathir's commentary. These righteous people spend their money through obeying God and give without expecting worldly return which is covered in verses 18 to 19.

The concept of Heaven and Hell is a recurring theme throughout the remainder of the Meccan period of Islam and into the Medinan period. In Chapter 7 verse 32 the good things of this life are for all, but the good things of the Hereafter are only for the believers. The rewards of the Hereafter are discussed again in Chapter 39 verse 10. In this verse rewards in the Hereafter are due to those who do good in this life. The exchange of the Hereafter for this life is also discussed in Chapter 42 verse 20. As discussed earlier, if one wishes for the Hereafter God will help him/her in this pursuit, but if s/he wants only this life then that will only be what they get based on the explanation of this verse by Ibn Kathir.

The concept of Rahman first developed in the first three years of Islam emphasized the Mercy of God despite the existence of both Heaven and Hell. The mercifulness of God is mentioned throughout the Qur'an and the traditions. In later Meccan verses this is also emphasized. In Chapter 7 verse 156 it is explained that God does as He pleases, but His Mercy is great. Further it is explained that His mercy is specifically for those who do good deeds, pay charity and believe in the revelations from God. In addition in Chapter 39 verses 53 to 54 the sinners are addressed in that the Mercy of God is always available to them, but a sinner must first repent to Him. Sinners are reassured in these verses that they should not despair of the Mercy of God.

2.6. Oneness of God

A major part of righteousness in Islam is belief in One God. One of the central chapters of the Qur'an regarding this issue was revealed in this early period. Chapter 112 was revealed when some idolaters asked the Prophet about God although Ibn Kathir indicated it could have been revealed in response to the Christians and Jews. If this is the case then this chapter would not have been revealed in Mecca. Either way, the primacy of this chapter in the Qur'an was reinforced by Ibn Kathir who reported that if one loves this chapter it will cause him/her to enter Heaven. The crux of the chapter is that God was not born nor does He give birth and nothing is like him.

The theme of the Oneness of God continues in the rest of the Meccan period. In Chapter 17 verse 42, it is made clear that God is alone in sovereignty in which there is no other god competing with Him. It is asserted in Chapter 21 verse 22 that God is alone in that if there were more than one God there would be destruction from competition between them. In Chapter 23 verse 91 the point about the level of confusion and destruction that would occur if there were multiple deities is reiterated. In this verse the issue of the lack of order from multiple deities is included along with their orientation to hoard power, try to control other gods and exercise their will over each other.

2.7. Patience in Adversity

The emphasis on patience in Islam started in this early period of revelation. In this early period the focus on patience is directed specifically
at the Prophet. In Chapter 93 the verses indicate that it was revealed,
at least part of it, in the initial period of very early revelation because
God was explaining to the Prophet that He was not displeased nor had
He forsaken him. This is probably in the time when there was no revelation for a while after the first revelation. In verse 5 in this chapter
God tells him that he would be pleased with what He would give him.

After this reassurance and emphasis on patience, God revealed to
him what he probably already knew, but needed to be reminded of to
reinforce his patience. He reminded the Prophet that he was an orphan
and He gave him shelter; he was wandering and He gave him guidance; he was dependent and He made him independent. God's reminder to the Prophet focused attention on the need to be patient with
God's plan.

2.8. The Marvels of Nature

God states in these early verses that He created everything and gave
His creation order and proportion in verse 2 of Chapter 87. Ibn Kathir
explained regarding this verse that God has created and fashioned
every creation in the best form. Human beings, a creation of God,
have also been created in the best form which is stated in verse 4 of
Chapter 95.

The form of human beings is described in its primordial phase to
emphasize the power of God as well as the meekness of mankind. In
Chapter 75 verses 37 to 39, God describes how the person goes from
sperm to clot to due proportions either as a male or female in the
womb before birth. As emphasized by Ibn Kathir, according to Islamic belief when the human being takes his/her form in the womb the
soul is then breathed into him/her.

The creation of God is focused on multiple times after the first
three years in the Qur'an. In the Meccan period it is mentioned several times. In Chapter 50 God declares that He created the Heavens and

the Earth in 6 *yawm* (periods / days) without getting tired. Further, it is explained in Chapter 21 verses 16 to 17 that He did not create these things (Heaven and Earth) for fun. Explaining this verse Ibn Kathir said that God created the Heavens and Earth in truth and justice and if He intended them for play He would not have created them. This is reiterated in Chapter 44 verses 38 to 39. In contrast, life and death were created to differentiate among men for the purposes of judgment as stressed in Chapter 67 verse 2 which was the topic covered earlier. The life of the Hereafter is stressed over the life of this world in which it is a higher and better state of creation as stated in Chapter 6 verse 32.

The creation of human beings from clay in this life is included in the later Meccan verses. In Chapter 15 verse 26 it is described how human beings were created from clay. Ibn Kathir added in his explanation of this verse that *jinns* were created from smokeless fire and angels were created from light. Both of these entities existed before humanity and more will be discussed on them later in this book.

2.9. Importance of Charity

In Chapter 107 verse 3 those that deny the Day of Judgment in the Hereafter are those who do not encourage the feeding of the poor. It is assumed that those who do not encourage this activity also do not do it and this action is related to their lack of faith. In addition, in the same chapter in verse 7 even the smallest of things such as lending an axe to someone who needs it is too much for those without faith. These characteristics are indicative of one who denies the Hereafter and his/her potential destination for not doing these things.

As already established in some of the earliest verses of the Qur'an, the later Meccan verses affirm the importance of charity in Islam. In Chapter 90 verses 11 to 17 the path of good is described as the path that is steep which gives salvation. Most of these verses focus on the giving of charity to the poor, in particular poor relatives, and this is considered something that is difficult to do, therefore it is a steep path. In Chapter 30 verse 38 the believers are commanded to give to their relatives and take care of the poor. Again, these actions are considered very important for salvation which in this verse means being able to see the face of God in the Hereafter according to Ibn Kathir.

Further, in the later Meccan verses the behavior of the believers is juxtaposed to the behavior of the unbelievers in Chapter 36 verse 47. In this verse the believers are commanded to spend on the poor while the unbelievers assert that they do not have a responsibility for the poor. They feel that the responsibility for the poor rests with God. Of course God is all-powerful and can do as He pleases, but each person is responsible for what God has given him/her and it is a great test to see what they will do with it. Giving to the poor is one of those actions that is considered very honorable in Islam and a method to attain the Hereafter.

2.10. Summary

In this chapter the major themes of the first three years of the revelation of the Qur'an are explored in detail. These major themes are prayer, the ephemeral nature of this life, the issue of death and resurrection, the Day of Judgment, Heaven and Hell, the Oneness of God, the virtue of patience, the reassurance to the Prophet, the marvels of nature and the importance of charity. These themes are not isolated to the first three years of the revelation of the Qur'an, but can be found throughout the Qur'an. These themes are the foundation of Islamic belief.

The importance of prayer is stressed in these verses as a means of purifying the soul and repelling evil. The pre-prayer ritual wash is also a major aspect of this purification. In these verses it is apparent that prayer is the first priority and one of the major reasons to observe prayer is for the remembrance of God.

Prayer is described as the first priority and seeking sustenance in this life is secondary, because another major theme in these early years is the ephemeral nature of this life. At this early stage of revelation, the Qur'an stresses that this life is beautiful, but temporary. The beauty of this life is a testament to the powers of God, which is also stressed in these early years of the Qur'an. Unfortunately, the priorities of people are in reverse where wealth acquisition is given a higher priority than the next life. This is why at this early stage of revelation the Qur'an states that the path of good is difficult while the path of evil is easy. It is stressed in these verses that God creates everything including the human being, and the whole purpose of life is not to acquire wealth, but good deeds which is the real currency of exchange in the next life.

In these early revelations people are reminded that they will die and they will be resurrected to face judgment when the good deeds will be weighed against the bad deeds. If there are more good deeds they will go to Heaven and if they have more bad deeds they will go to Hell. God's wonderful Mercy is not absent in this absolute result, as described in this early period. The whole argument is a circle in which good deeds are accumulated through worship to God, who is stressed as the only God in these early revelations and throughout the Qur'an. A major part of those good deeds is doing charity which is emphasized in one of the first verses of the Qur'an. These things are not easy, of course, so God stresses to his Prophet, and indirectly to those who believe, that patience is important and that God's Plan is not easy to comprehend nor does it happen quickly from the perspective of people.

CHAPTER 3

THE FIRST THREE YEARS THEMES AND JESUS

The First Three Years Themes and Jesus

T he themes in the first three years of Islam can also be found in the Gospels. As already mentioned there is debate over the length of time Jesus preached ranging from one year or less to three years. The standard assumption appears to be that he preached for three years before he departed from this world. This timeframe coincides with the length of time that Muhammad preached before Islam was publicly preached and the oppression of the Muslims began in Mecca.

As previously mentioned, the four canonical Gospel books (Matthew, Mark, Luke and John) are considered the teachings of Jesus and other books in the New Testament are not considered here. The Protestant Bible (New International Version) and the Catholic Bible (The New American Version) serve as the sources for these four books of the Gospel. All quotations in this chapter are taken from the New International Version.

3.1. Only One God

There are a number of teachings in the Gospel that clearly indicate that God is One and only One. In Mark 12:29 after Jesus was asked which commandment is the most important he replied that, "the most important one, answered Jesus, is this: 'Hear, O Israel: The Lord our God, The Lord is one.'"[25] Another similar story involves a lawyer in Luke 10:25 who asked Jesus what he should do to receive eternal life as a means to test him. Jesus asked him in a rhetorical manner how the lawyer read the law. The lawyer responded with some commandments

---

[25] International Bible Society. (1984). *The Bible: New International Version*. Colorado Springs, CO: International Bible Society. (p. 1069).

including the requirement to love God with all of one's heart. Jesus responded in verse 28 that he had answered correctly. This same story appears in Matthew 22:37 and Mark 12:31.

In Matthew 4:10 Jesus was confronted by the Devil who tempted him that he would give him all the kingdoms of the world if he worshiped him. Jesus responded that it is written that you should worship and serve God alone. In addition in Matthew 6:24 an analogy of two masters is used that shows that one can only serve one master. It describes the relationships that develop when one has two masters. One he serves and another he hates. In this verse the two masters are God and money. This verse is repeated in Luke 16:13.

There are some verses in the Gospel that make it clear that nothing is like God indicating His uniqueness much like the conception of God in Islam. In Mark 10:18 Jesus responded to someone calling him good in which he said that none are good except God alone. In Mark 10:27 Jesus asserted that nothing is impossible with God. In Matthew 23:9 Jesus exhorted his followers not to call anyone one's father in that everyone has only one father who is God.

3.2. Charity

Charity is emphasized in the religions of Islam and Christianity. It was one of the themes of the first three years of Islam and it was a theme of the ministry of Jesus. In Matthew 19:21 Jesus recommended to a rich man seeking the next life that he should sell what he has and give it to the poor. This strong advice is repeated in Mark 10:21.

The theme of giving without expecting return emphasized in the Qur'an and the first three years of the mission of Muhammad is repeated in the four books of the Gospel. In Luke 14:13-14 advice is given that feasts should be open to the poor and disabled in which the repayment for this service will be at the resurrection, i.e. Judgment Day. The giving of charity is also compensated for in the Hereafter in the Qur'an.

Another verse that emphasizes the reward in the Hereafter given to those who give charity is in Luke 6:35. In this verse the giving of charity is described as lending without return. The reward in return is described as great including being elevated to the status of sons of God. The use of the term 'path that is steep' in the Qur'an regarding actions that receive this reward is also reproduced in the Gospels. In Matthew 7:13 it is stated that the narrow gate is the gate that one should enter while the broad gate is the gate that leads to destruction. The use of the term narrow indicates that it is difficult to pass through that way whereas the term broad indicates that it is easy to pass that direction. Giving charity is one of those difficult ways, but the eventual reward is great.

The giving of charity without seeking recognition in this life is a concept in both Islam and Christianity as already discussed in Chapter 107 of the Qur'an. According to Khalil Jassemm in his book *Islamic Perspective on Charity: A Comprehensive Guide for Running a Muslim Nonprofit in the U.S.* he states that, "Islam teaches that giving privately is highly favorable over drawing attention to one's charitable acts."[26] He cites a *hadith* which states, "Allah loves the pious rich man, who (in spite of his piety and wealth) is obscure and unknown to fame (in *Sahih* Muslim)."[27]

In Matthew 6:3 an analogy to giving secretly is used. It states that one gives with his right hand in such secrecy that even the left hand does not know what is happening. Verse 4 confirms that the reason for making this analogy is to emphasize that giving should be secret. This same analogy is used in Islam. A *hadith* reported in *Sahih* Bukhari (Volume 2, Book 24, #504) states that there will be seven classes of people who will receive God's Mercy on the Day of Judgment. One of those classes of people are those who give secretly so that the left hand does not know what the right hand has given in charity.[28]

---

26 Jassemm, K. (2006). *Islamic Perspective on Charity: A Comprehensive Guide for Running a Muslim Nonprofit in the U.S.* Bloomington, IN: AuthorHouse. (p. 23).

27 Ibid. p. 23.

28 *Sahih* Bukhari. (n.d.). Retrieved from www.sahih-bukhari.com/.

3.3. Prayer

Prayer is a critical aspect of faith in Islam and Christianity. It was the first emphasis in the first three years of Islam in Mecca. It is also found in the Gospels in the New Testament. In Mark 1:35 Jesus got up early while it was still dark and prayed. This is similar to the night prayer instituted in the first three years of Islam in Mecca. Jesus prayed again in Matthew 26:37-39 when he was distraught. He then fell on his face and prayed. Praying in this way, i.e. prostration, is known as *sujud* in Arabic and was instituted in Islamic prayer in the first three years. *Sujud*, or the placing of the face on the ground in prayer, is part of many religious traditions not only Islam and Christianity.

In Matthew 6:5 there is advice that prayer should be in secret because the hypocrites were known to pray publicly so they would be seen. In Islam this advice is also given as discussed in Chapter 107 in the Qur'an, but it does not forbid public prayer. In Islam prayer has to flow from pure intentions whether in public or private. This is called *ikhlas*. This is the intention of the verse in Matthew despite its focus on the method to ensure sincerity of prayer.

The answering of prayers is just as important a topic today as it was at the time of Jesus and Muhammad. It is covered in the teachings of Jesus in Luke 11:10. In this verse, it is stressed that those who ask of God will receive from Him. Further, this verse uses the analogy of a door in which the one who knocks on it will receive an answer from God. This indicates that one must be proactive in seeking God's help in which He is always ready to open the door and assist the believer. This is also found in the Qur'an. A later Meccan chapter/verse 40:60 emphasizes that the believer should call upon God and He will answer him/her.

3.4. Patience

Patience in the teachings of the Prophet Muhammad in the first three years revolves around the challenges he faced when experiencing revelation for the first time. Later after the first three years the issue of patience focused on the oppressions experienced by Muhammad and the early

Muslim converts by the tribes of Mecca. These oppressions reflect the oppressions experienced by Jesus and his followers by the Israelite tribes in Palestine. The verses in the Gospels reflect this reality.

In Mark 13:13 it is prophesized that the believers will be hated at the end of times, but there is advice that one should endure to be saved. This endurance with the hardships experienced by those who dare to believe is further communicated through a well-known injunction in Christianity: love your enemy. In Luke 6:35 it is emphasized that one should love one's enemies. In Matthew 5:44 it is recommended to love your enemies and pray for those that persecute you. In Luke 6:27 the same injunction to love your enemies is made along with doing good to those who hate you. It is repeated in verse 35 of the same chapter.

The most famous set of verses in the Gospels that emphasize the need for patience in the face of hatred is in Matthew 5:39. It is recommended that if one slaps you, you are to turn your other cheek. It is hard to imagine this passivity in practice, but this standard of patience is also to be found in the Qur'an. Later in discussions on forgiveness we will touch upon this topic again. There is a huge emphasis on forgiveness in the Qur'an, however, this is usually disregarded by critics, who unfairly accuse Islam on this matter.

3.5. Hereafter

In the four books of the Gospel there are references to the goal of the Hereafter, i.e. Heaven. The most pronounced verses in this regard are in Matthew 6:19-21. These verses stress the importance of putting one's treasure in the Hereafter and not in this life. The treasures in this life are subject to decay and theft whereas the treasures in the next life are eternal. These verses are repeated in concept in Luke 12:33-34.

The treasures for the Hereafter are obviously not the same as the treasures in this life. The treasures in this life are possessions as pointed out in Luke 12:33. The treasure in the next life is Heaven which comes from belief. This is confirmed in John 5:24. In this verse, belief in God will lead one to eternal life. This importance of belief to reach

Heaven is in the Qur'an as well. As already mentioned, Chapter 7 verse 32 notes that the rewards of Heaven are only for those who believe.

The believer is expected to be oriented towards Heaven more so than to this life. In John 12:25 it is stated, "The man who loves his life will lose it, while the man who hates his life in this world will keep it for eternal life."[29] This idea has a counterpart in the Qur'an in Chapter 42 verse 20 which states, "To any that desires the tilth of the Hereafter, We give increase in his tilth, and to any that desires the tilth of this world, We grant somewhat thereof, but he has not share or lot in the Hereafter."[30] These verses indicate that there is an exchange between this life and the Hereafter where one cannot fully have both.

The means to achieve the Hereafter besides belief is through following God's commands and implementing His Will. This concept is firmly established in Islam. Even the name for one who believes in Islam is a Muslim which means one who submits his will to the Will of God. In Matthew 7:21 Jesus stressed that those who do the Will of God will enter Heaven. The Will of God is usually captured in His commandments. In Matthew 19:17 Jesus stated that one enters 'life' by following the commandments. Throughout the Gospel, 'life' means the Hereafter i.e. eternal life in Heaven.

One of the incentives to follow the commands of God is the fear of His punishment. The fear of God or God-consciousness in Islam is known as *taqwa* in Arabic. It is also a concept in the Gospels. In Luke 12:4-5 Jesus warned that the believer is not to fear those who 'kill the body,' but fear God who can kill and send to Hell.

3.6. God's Mercy

The Mercy of God is the hope that He will forgive sins, save mankind from Hell and relieve the oppressed and sick in this life. This concept is one of the initial concepts of God in Islam as previously explained. It is also a concept that can be found in the Gospels.

---

[29] International Bible Society, 1984, op.cit. (p. 1150).
[30] Ali, A. Y. (2010). *The Meaning of the Glorious Qur'an*. Istanbul, Turkey: ASIR Media. (p. 329).

There are two accounts of the Mercy of God in the Gospels. In Matthew 21:31-37, Jesus concluded his story of the two sons by noting that even the tax collectors and the prostitutes will go to Heaven sometimes even over those who may be deemed righteous. The reason for this is because they truly believed in God and His Prophets, in this case, the Prophet John, while those who supposedly follow God's Law rejected some of the Prophets including John. The Mercy of God extends to all as this verse reveals.

Even those who may not believe, but treat the believers well may receive the Mercy of God. At the time of Jesus this may have been a reference to the Samaritans and Greeks/Romans, who were considered unbelievers. Jesus explained in Mark 9:41 that the one who helps someone because they are a believer will receive his reward from God. In both of these cases the Mercy of God is translated into acceptance into Heaven.

3.7. Judgment Day

The knowledge of the Day of Judgment when people will be sorted into Heaven or Hell is not known of its exact timing except with God. This is a fact that is established in both the Qur'an and the Gospels. In Matthew 24:36 it establishes that no one even the angels or Jesus know when the Day of Judgment will be.

When the Day of Judgment does occur it will be a time when all people will be held accountable for their actions. This is established in the Qur'an and the Gospels. In Matthew 12:36 even the words the people have spoken will be a cause for them to be condemned.

3.8. Summary

The purpose of this chapter is to compare the resonating teachings of the Qur'an in the first three years of revelation with the teachings of the Gospel. As discussed above there are many teachings that are the same or similar. For instance, the idea that God is one and unique in which all is possible with Him is the same between the Qur'an and the Gospels. Jesus described this as the most important commandment, i.e. to love and praise the one God.

The teachings of Jesus and Muhammad also resonate with the giving of charity in which the idea is described by both men as lending without return in which the return will be the good reward of the Hereafter or in Christian theology the rewards will be in the Hereafter. The virtue of giving in secret, i.e. giving without seeking fame, is praised in both the teachings of Muhammad and Jesus. At the heart of this concern is being sincere in the giving of charity in which both Jesus and Muhammad stress this sincerity in all the acts of worship in which the orientation has to be towards praising God. Jesus stressed this so much in fact that besides giving charity in secret he recommends praying in secret to maintain this sincerity in worship.

The centrality of worship is stressed in the Qur'an and the Gospels. Jesus prayed at night and by placing his face on the ground just like Muhammad was commanded to do in the first three years of revelation. The issue of prayers being answered was a concern for both Jesus and Muhammad while both of these men taught and were taught to be patient, although in the first three years of Muhammad's mission this patience was specifically regarding the unfolding of the plan of God. In the later period in Mecca this patience took on the same qualities as that taught by Jesus because of the public preaching of Islam.

The emphasis on the next world over this world can be found in the teachings of these two great men. The next world has treasures that are greater than any treasure in this world, but to gain those treasures one has to believe and follow the commands of God. The centrality of proper belief can be found in the Qur'an and the Gospels. This is not to say that the Mercy of God is not stressed in both of these books in which His Mercy extends to all people. Despite this Mercy, the Day of Judgment is a reality in both of these holy books. The timing of this event is known by no one save God.

Most, if not all, of the teachings of Muhammad in the first three years as codified in the Qur'an are comparable to the teachings of Jesus during his Prophetic career which spanned the same time period. One of the differences is the orientation of the teaching of patience in which Jesus was publicly preaching from the beginning of his mission while Muhammad only did so after the first three years. Jesus taught his followers to turn the other cheek and pray for forgiveness for their oppressors while these concepts did not surface until after the public preaching of Islam in Mecca when the leaders of the city began torturing the Muslims to get them to renounce their religion. This is the later period of Meccan revelations which is discussed in the following chapters.

CHAPTER 4

THE LAST 10 YEARS
IN MECCA

The Last 10 Years in Mecca

The last ten years in Mecca after the first three years of initial revelation were trying years both for the Prophet and his followers. There was much oppression against the Muslims in those years and the catalyst for that oppression was the public preaching of Islam. Verses 94 to 97 in Chapter 15 gave the order to proclaim the commands of God.[31]

One of the first efforts towards public preaching involved a meal with the Prophet's tribesmen, the *Bani* Abd Al-Muttalib. The first meal was interrupted by Abu Lahab, an avowed enemy of Muhammad and one of his uncles. The second meal did not go any better with his tribesmen rejecting his claims to Prophethood and even laughing at him.[32]

Although many enemies of the Prophet contemplated his murder, such as one of his worst enemies, Abu Jahl, the protection of Abu Talib, the Prophet's uncle and head of his tribe, prevented them from doing this. Instead they attacked the followers of Muhammad who did not have these protections while they worked to defame him. They accused him of being a madman, possessed, a poet and a sorcerer. They made sure to spread these defamations far and wide which eventually reached the tribes of Yathrib.[33]

The level of insult reached a point where Hamza, another uncle of Muhammad, could take it no longer and defended the Prophet while

---

[31] Quran Tafsir Ibn Kathir - Home. (2010, March). Retrieved from www.qtafsir.com/
[32] Guillaume, A. (2002). *The Life of Muhammad (M. Al-Saqqa, I. Al-Abyari, & A.H. Shalabi)*. New York, NY: Oxford Uni. Press. (Original work published 1937).
[33] Ibid.

embracing Islam in the process. Most of the men in Mecca feared Hamza which led one of the leaders of Mecca to make an offer to Muhammad to halt his preaching of Islam. Utbah b. Rabia offered money, honor, and sovereignty. These were all rejected in which Muhammad then recited part of Chapter 41 which made a major impact on Utbah.[34]

Another strategy of the leaders of Mecca was to attempt to delegitimize his assertion of Prophethood and his message. The leaders sent a delegation to Yathrib, later known as Medina, to ask the Jewish tribes there if they could help to invalidate him as a Prophet. They recommended that they should ask him three questions which if he was unable to answer then he was not a true Prophet. These questions concerned the "men in the cave," the traveler named Dhul-Qarnayn, and the Spirit. When these questions were put to Muhammad he deferred the answer to revelation which came several days later. These revelations can be found in Chapter 18 and Chapter 17.[35]

In addition, they accused him of learning his revelations from an informant. One of them was a man they thought was called al-Rahman from al-Yamama, who probably did not exist because the pagan Arabs probably mistook the name al-Rahman (The Most Merciful) for a name of a person and not God. Another was a man called Jabr, who was a Christian slave who did not speak Arabic very well. These accusations bore no fruit. The leaders of Mecca continued their physical abuses on his followers anyway.[36]

These abuses prompted the first migration of the Muslims out of Mecca to Abyssinia or present-day Ethiopia. The leaders of Mecca wanted to bring these first immigrants back so they sent two representatives to the leadership of Abyssinia to influence them to return Muslims to Mecca. They bribed the generals in an effort to influence the Abyssinia leader called The Negus. They also stirred trouble for the Muslim immigrants by pointing out to these Monophysite Christians

---

[34] Ibid.

[35] Ibid.

[36] Ibid.

that they rejected the divinity of Jesus.[37] The Monophysite Christians believed Jesus was wholly divine and not a man at all except in image.[38]

At this time in Christian history there were three major groups of Christians. There were those that believed Jesus was only a man although still holy as believed by the Arians. There were those that believed Jesus was both divine and a man, which is the belief of contemporary Christians. There were those that believed Jesus was only divine in which he only appeared as a man, which was the belief of the Monophysite Christians.[39]

The immigrant Muslims were confronted about their beliefs regarding Jesus. Ja'far, an eloquent speaker sent with the immigrants for that reason, recited part of Chapter 19 and the story on Mary and Jesus contained there. The Negus responded after hearing this, "Of a truth, this and what Jesus brought have come from the same niche."[40] Further, regarding the Muslim conception of Jesus, the Negus added, "By God, Jesus, son of Mary, does not exceed what you have said by the length of this stick."[41] These statements by the Negus created considerable discontent towards him especially by his generals and his people but the Muslim immigrants stayed in Abyssinia despite the best efforts of the leaders of Mecca.[42]

The turbulence for the Muslims that stayed behind in Mecca continued after this first migration. Shortly after Umar converted to Islam, which was a great asset for this early Muslim community, the leaders of Mecca sanctioned the *Bani* Hashim and the *Bani* Muttalib. These tribes included most of the Muslims including the Prophet Muhammad. Many of the Arabs refused to accept a Prophet who was not of their own tribe. This is one of the reasons Abu Jahl rejected Muhammad so vehemently. These sanctions included a prohibition on

---

[37] Ibid.

[38] Jenkins, P. (2010). *Jesus Wars: How Four Patriarchs, Three Queens, and Two Emperors Decided What Christians Would Believe for the Next 1,500 Years*. New York, New York: HarperOne.

[39] Ibid.

[40] Guillaume, 2002, op.cit. (p. 152).

[41] Ibid (p. 152).

[42] Lings, 2006, op.cit.

marriage to them and no buying and selling with them. These sanctions remained in force for two or three years. In the course of this boycott, the Prophet's wife, Khadija, passed away and then the uncle of Muhammad, Abu Talib, also passed away. When Abu Talib died he was replaced as tribal leader by Abu Lahab who hated Muhammad. The tribal protection for Muhammad effectively stopped after this event.[43]

In an effort to secure some protection the Prophet traveled to Taif, a strong town not far from Mecca. The response of the leadership of Taif was negative towards his requests for protection. They attacked him by stoning him out of the town. After his return from Taif, Mut'im ibn Adiyy offered his protection and this secured Muhammad until Mut'im's death.[44]

The Heavenly Night Journey occurred after this in which the Prophet traveled to Jerusalem and then to Heaven. In Heaven he met the previous Prophets and he received the commands to pray five times a day. After his return, Muhammad declared his journey publicly. What he was telling was so miraculous that while it was rejected outright by disbelievers, it was not easy to fathom even for some Muslims. Abu Bakr was not one of these in which he confirmed that if the Prophet said it then it was true. Abu Bakr earned the title *al-Saddiq* which means the one who testifies to the truth as a result of his affirmations of Muhammad's declarations about the Night Journey.[45]

After this, the Prophet began meeting with delegations from a town in the north at that time called Yathrib. Eventually Mus'ab ibn Umayr went to Yathrib to spread Islam. The people of this city were extremely divided with many wars that were tearing their city apart. They were looking for a leader and their interest in Muhammad began early in his mission starting when the leaders of Mecca sent representatives to the Jewish tribes of Yathrib to ask about Muhammad's claims.[46]

---

43   Ibid.
44   Ibid.
45   Guillaume, 2002, op.cit.
46   Ibid.

Eventually the Muslims began immigrating to Yathrib, or what later became known as Medina. This immigration is known as the *hijra*. When Mut'im died the Prophet also migrated. This occurred not a second too soon as the leaders of Mecca had planned to kill the Prophet while he slept in his bed. He was gone before they got there and despite pursuing him they were unable to stop him from reaching Medina.[47] This began the Medinan period of Islam.

The following chapters represent the largest section of Qur'anic verses in this book. It is divided into five separate chapters in which each chapter is split into two sections. The first section contains Qur'anic verses that resonate with verses in the Gospel and the second section contains Qur'anic verses that stand alone without a counterpart in the Gospel.

Chapter 5 revolves around verses that focus on the unbelievers. Chapter 6 focuses on the commands. These are the verses that have rules in them for the Muslim community to follow. Chapter 7 pertains to the rewards of God on mankind. These verses emphasize God's Mercy on mankind and the bounties He showers upon them. Chapter 8 contains all the stories and parables found in the Meccan period. These include some stories known in other traditions such as Christianity and stories that are unique to the Qur'an. Lastly, chapter 9 is a group of explanations which explain things such as pre-destination and the creation.

---

[47] Ibid.

CHAPTER 5

THE ISSUE OF DISBELIEF

The Issue of Disbelief

This chapter is focused on those verses / teachings that address the issue of disbelief and disbelievers. During the lives of Muhammad and Jesus this was a constant issue that merited instruction for those who believed in their messages and the One God. The role of those who did not believe in generating these verses was substantial since their behaviors had a major impact on these early communities of believers. After all, it was a community of unbelievers that led to the trials of Jesus and Muhammad in their respective communities.

As mentioned in the previous chapter, this chapter is split into two major sections in which the first section highlights verses/teachings that have counterparts between the Qur'an and the Gospels. Since this is the focus of this book this is the first section in this chapter. The second section highlights verses/teachings that can only be found in the Qur'an, but do not conflict with any of the verses/teachings in the Gospels. Each of these sections has several sub-sections some of which are repeated in the second section with verses that do not have counterparts in the Gospels.

5.1. The Issue of Disbelief: The Qur'an and the Gospels

The Qur'an and the Gospels have several verses that address a multitude of issues surrounding disbelief. The first group of these verses focuses on the results of not believing in the One God and the message that these Prophets brought to their people and the world. This group of verses is split into those where the results occur in this life and those that occur in the next life. The second group of verses addresses the claims of those who did not believe at the time of Muhammad and

Jesus. The unbelievers made several claims that initiated these teach-
ings/verses. The third group of verses list different facts about disbelief
that are important to know for the believers.

5.1.1. Earthly Results of Disbelief

In this first group of verses the results of disbelief in the One God and
His message are seen in this world. As mentioned earlier, those who
transgress are actually provided with many seemingly great things of this
life such as wealth, power and possessions which only cause them to go
more astray. Although they may be implicitly aware of this, the Devil is
constantly working to make sure they continue in their transgression
and remain stubborn regarding the messages of the Prophets so much
so that they demand new messages to affirm what they want in this life
versus what they should want in this life which is what the Prophets
bring with them. These issues are discussed separately in this section.

Punishment in the Form of Provision and Respite

In Chapter 6 verse 44, the concept of earthly reward for rejecting the
guidance of God is established. Ibn Kathir explained that people
ignore the warning of God which causes Him to open all the gates of
provision for them. They receive wealth, children, and provisions
thinking it is a blessing from God when in reality it is a curse. As noted
in Chapter 17 verse 18, God will give to whom He pleases, those who
desire this life in exchange for the next. These good things are an illusion which becomes apparent when God calls them to account.

Once the warning of God becomes fulfilled, those who ignored it
will then realize their mistake, which is identified in Chapter 19 verse
75. The fulfillment of the warning though could occur over a long
period of time. In Chapter 21 verse 44, it is explained that God
deceives those who do not believe in Him by giving them luxuries and
a long life while the territory under the control of disbelief slowly loses
ground to belief. In addition, they will think that the incoming punishment is a blessing as explained in Chapter 68 verse 44.

In an effort to show that God's design is not to mislead mankind it is
explained in Chapter 43 verses 33 to 35 that if it was not for the general

belief and confusion over wealth as a sign of the Mercy of God, He would have given all those who stray from Him ladders and staircases made of silver, i.e. great wealth. Ibn Kathir explained that the value of this life is not high in God's estimation whereas for the unbelievers things such as silver are more valuable than the Hereafter. Ibn Kathir further explained from a *hadith* that if this world had any value even of a gnat's wing, then God would not give a disbeliever a single drink of water.

Far from wealth being an indication of disobedience alone in Chapter 89 it is explained that all of this, whether one is in wealth or poverty, is a test. Wealth is a test like poverty. Ibn Kathir explained that God gives to those He loves and those He does not love, and no one should feel that wealth is a sign of that love. This logic is counter to Protestant understandings of wealth.[48]

The rejection of wealth as an indication of God's Blessing is clearly stated in Chapter 34 verse 37 in which it is stated that wealth and children are not a sign of God's love for the wealthy. Ibn Kathir cited a *hadith* of the Prophet Muhammad in relation to his explanation of this verse in which it was recorded that Abu Hurayrah said that the Prophet said, "God does not look at your outward appearance or your wealth, rather He looks at your hearts and your deeds."[49] The arrogance of some people who are wealthy meant that at the time of the Prophet and before him the wealthy usually disbelieved in the message brought from God while the poor and weak followed it. This fact is stated in Chapter 34 verse 34.

The teachings of Jesus are more pronounced regarding wealth and the possibilities for wealthy individuals to receive Heaven in the Hereafter. In Matthew 19:23-24 and in Mark 10:25 it is stated that it is exceptionally difficult for a rich person to enter Heaven. An analogy of a camel passing through the eye of a needle being easier than a rich person entering Heaven is used to highlight the difficulty. This same

---

[48] Bénabou, R., &Tirole, J. (2006). Belief in a just world and redistributive politics. *Quarterly Journal of Economics*, 121(2), 699-746; Nash, J. A. (1995). Toward the Revival and Reform of the Subversive Virtue: Frugality. *The Annual of the Society of Christian Ethics*, 15, 137-160; Fitzgerald, C. S. (2011). Looking Back to Move Forward: Christian Social Thought, Religious Traditionalism, and Welfare Theory. *Social Work & Christianity*, 38(3), 267-292.

[49] Quran Tafsir Ibn Kathir - Home. (2010, March). Retrieved from www.qtafsir.com/.

analogy is used in the Qur'an in Chapter 7 verse 40, but it is directed at those who do not believe, whether they are rich or poor.

Benefits from the Qur'an Are Difficult to Ascertain

There are some people who are so entrenched with their rejection of the guidance from God that the message never reaches their heart. In 6:25 the phrase 'We have thrown veils on their hearts' emphasizes how they have been prevented from ever hearing it and receiving any benefits from it because of their ill-intentions and arrogance. All they can do is dispute over the message and with the Prophet that brings the message.

In Chapter 36 verse 11 it is stated that only the believers will benefit from the warning in the Qur'an. This means that they follow the Qur'an and benefit from its injunctions. In addition, they are aware that God always sees them, He will forgive their sins and they will achieve Paradise so long as they follow the Qur'an. This belief and assurance is a great benefit for those that believe in it.

Ibn Kathir added that disbelievers do not believe in any of the signs for belief. They also say heinous things about Muhammad such as he forged it. In addition to their rejection and accusations they also work to keep others from hearing the message as well.

In the teachings of Jesus the reality that God's message can only be heard by those who accept guidance from God can be found in John 8:47 in which whoever is of God, i.e. those who obey Him and believe in Him, can hear the words of God while those who cannot hear the words of God are not of Him. This point is illustrated in Matthew 11:25 when Jesus thanked God for keeping His Truth hidden from the wise and understanding, but revealing it to little children. Intelligence and experience is no substitute for the pure heart which children embody before the eyes of God. Mankind should strive for that purity.

Those Who Abuse the Prophets and Their Punishment

In Chapter 17 verse 77 it is asserted that there is a way things happen with all the Messengers, that has not changed with any of them throughout time. In the previous verse, 76, it is noted that the unbelievers aim to chase the Muslims off their land, but they will not remain on that land for long. Ibn Kathir explained that God punishes those who chase their Prophets out of their towns/country. He also noted that it could mean killing them, which is what happened to the people of Lot. Further, he added that this is something that God does in this situation.

The teachings of Jesus also address this topic. In Luke 11:47 the tribes of Israel are rebuked for their treatment of the Prophets in former generations in which the generation at the time of Jesus was not different in their treatment of him. Later in Luke 11:50-51 Jesus stated that the blood of the Prophets would be charged against this generation which referred to the generation living at the time of Jesus.

The People Are Led Astray by Satan

The remembrance of God is very important in Islam. In Chapter 43 verse 36 the people who stop remembering God and turn away from Him are lost. Further, those who do so receive a devil that is sent from God to lead this person astray. In this regard the best way to shake this evil one is to remember God. In Arabic this is called *dhikr* or the remembering of God. Muslims are advised to do it as much as possible.

Jesus in the Gospels also pointed out that there are some men that are so lost that their will becomes the will of the Devil. In John 8:44 Jesus accused those who rejected him of being of the Devil and given to his will. These people were unable to hear and understand the truth that Jesus brought to them because they were more apt to turn to the whisperings of the Devil who is really the greatest liar.

5.1.2. Hereafter Results of Disbelief

The previous section describes some of the earthly results of disbelief included in the Meccan verses. This section focuses on the Hereafter results of disbelief. These are different than the previous section. One obvious result is Hell which was discussed a little in the previous section. In particular those who died in a state of disbelief will regret this, realize that what they worshipped besides God was false, be denied Heaven, and be forgotten. Lastly, those who were once believers, but had fallen out of belief will also receive punishment.

Just by these brief descriptions one can see how different these results are with the earthly results discussed previously. The stakes are higher in the Hereafter.

The Unbelievers Will Be Forgotten by God

It may be the greatest torment described in the Qur'an for those in Hell. In Chapter 7 verse 51 the unbelievers will be forgotten by God in their torments in Hell. Ibn Kathir noted that there are various interpretations of this verse, but it is hard to believe that the All-Knowing God actually forgets them. This may mean that they are treated like they are forgotten which is the interpretation of Ibn Kathir.

In the earthly life all people can feel assured that God hears their prayers and are not forgotten by Him. The world may forget them, but God does not forget them. This is a consolation for people especially when they are in trouble and alone. In Hell, the greatest trouble that anyone will ever face, they will not even have this consolation.

Jesus similarly taught that in this life the rich, the hunger-free, those who laugh and those who are well-respected in this life will have their consolations while they are still alive as presented in Luke 6:24-26. These consolations will not follow them in the Hereafter as Jesus was pronouncing woe upon them. It can only be assumed that Jesus was referring to those who were rich, hunger-free, jolly and respected and were not grateful for the benefits that God had given them in this life. Ungratefulness would be rejecting Him and His Commands. In Christianity it would be a rejection of the blessings that Jesus brought from God.

The Punishment of God on Apostates

In Chapter 16 verses 106 to 107, but especially verse 106 since 107 refers back to this verse, there is the expression of God's anger towards those who leave the faith of Islam after having established it. In verse 106 it is emphasized that they will receive severe punishment in the Hereafter. This punishment is the torments of Hell.

Further, as explained by Ibn Kathir this exempts those who were forced to leave their religion under threat. This may include the thousands of Muslims forcibly converted during the Spanish Reconquista. There are more examples of this in history, but even at the earliest time of Islam in Mecca the leaders of Mecca were successful in forcibly converting back some Muslims through torture. However, in Islam, Muslims are allowed to pretend they were converted out of Islam under torture or threat while they were keeping their Islamic faith in secret. This is a permissible behavior for a while.

The issue of apostasy was also apparent in the time of Jesus. In John 6:66 after Jesus made it clear that only those granted permission by God can approach him, many of his disciples walked away from him. Even amongst the remaining 12 disciples according to Christian doctrine one of them, Judas, betrayed Jesus as mentioned in verses 70 to 71. Even in the final hours of Jesus in the Gospels the disciples faded away, such as Peter who denied Jesus during his trials as mentioned in John 13:38 and John 18:17.

5.1.3. Claims of the Unbelievers

In this section the unbelievers make claims based on their mere conjecture and desires. At the time of the Prophet they made claims about the Prophet, questioned his legitimacy, and doubted in the truth of what he brought to the people of Mecca. One of the strategies of the unbelievers in every era is to delegitimize the man who brought the message. The contemporaries of Jesus made these types of accusations about him. It is amazing today these same accusations have not disappeared and is one of the main reasons for this book.

Claims about the Prophet

One of the major claims about Muhammad was that he either invented the message or learned it from someone else. These claims are addressed in the Qur'an. In Chapter 25 verses 4 to 6 the claims that he invented the message and/or asked others to help him are highlighted. Their aim in making this claim was to expose Muhammad as a fake, but verse 4 states that it is them who were false. Further in verse 6 it is reinforced that the Qur'an was sent down by God.

The same claim is addressed in Chapter 16 verse 103 in which the leaders of Mecca stated that the Prophet was taught by a foreign man who used to sell goods in Mecca around al-Safa. Muhammad was seen talking to him sometimes. In this verse this argument is rejected because this foreign merchant knew only a little Arabic while the Qur'an was revealed in Arabic.

Another claim by the unbelievers in Mecca at this time was that Muhammad was crazy. In Chapter 44 verse 14 they again made the claim that he was taught by others and they added that he was a madman or possessed. This is also addressed in Chapter 68 verse 2 where the Prophet was reassured that he was not mad or possessed.

At the time of Jesus, the Pharisees also accused Jesus of being in league with the Devil and further being possessed by an evil spirit. In John 8:48 the Pharisees accused Jesus of being a Samaritan, a nomenclature for a heretic, and possessed by a demon. They made this claim again in Matthew 9:34 and again in Matthew 12:24-25 in which Jesus' ability to cast out demons was associated with help from the Devil himself, i.e. that he was in league with the Devil.

The Pharisees also could not understand how Jesus knew what he knew since he had not studied previously as stated in John 7:15-16. In verse 16 Jesus responded that the teaching is not his, but God's teaching. This is the same rebuttal in the Qur'an towards the Meccan leaders who also wondered how Muhammad came upon the knowledge that he displayed in the verses of the Qur'an.

Prophets Should Not Eat

This is considered separately from the previous section on the claims about the Prophet because it represents a general belief about Prophets that the Meccans had at the time. They asked about the Prophet's need to eat and work. It was their assumption that a Prophet was a god-like entity that had help from the angels in delivering his message which could be visually seen by men.

This assumption about Prophets was not only held by the Meccans but many other people around the Middle East. This is refuted several times in the Qur'an both for Muhammad as well as the Prophets that came before him in Chapter 25 verse 7. This claim is also found in the Gospels in Matthew 11:19 in which the Pharisees accused Jesus of being a fake because he ate, drank and made friends with tax collectors and sinners.

The Message Should Be Revealed to Someone Greater

One of the reasons that people expected Prophets to be god-like is because they expected the Messenger to be as powerful or worthy of worship as the one who sent the message, i.e. God. Even within their societies many of those who stepped forward to bring a message were of the lower strata of their society. Muhammad was not of the lowest strata, but he was not the elite of Mecca or the region. It is for this reason that in Chapter 43 verse 31 these ideas / claims are addressed.

The unbelievers questioned why the message was not sent to one of the leaders in the two prominent towns in the area. These towns were Mecca and Taif. Taif was the town as discussed in the history of the Meccan period where the Prophet traveled to seek protection after his uncle died and Abu Lahab, his avowed enemy and another uncle, gained control of the tribe. He was stoned out of the city.

In the next verse, 32, it is emphasized that the message was given to whom God chose. As explained by Ibn Kathir this message was to be given to one who was the purest of heart and soul. This man was Muhammad amongst his people.

This was an issue at the time of Jesus. In Matthew 13:55 and Mark 6:4, the Pharisees are flabbergasted at the claims of Jesus since before that they knew him as the carpenter's son. The rejection of Jesus because of his family's background or their familiarity with his family caused Jesus to make the very realistic claim that Prophets are never honored in their hometown in Luke 4:24, Matthew 13:57 and John 4:44. The Meccans never accepted Muhammad until the power of Islam became so overwhelming that out of opportunity they embraced it. The same could easily be said about Christianity in the Roman and Greek world including Palestine where Jesus was rejected and oppressed.

Think They Will Never Be Resurrected

Finally, beyond the unbeliever's claims about Prophethood and specifically the Prophet, they also made claims that counter the message that was being brought to them. It is emphasized in Islam as it is in Christianity that there will be a Judgment Day where the dead will be resurrected to face this judgment. In Chapter 51 verses 10 to 14 there is a strong refutation to this idea. It is pointed out in these verses by Ibn Kathir that the unbelievers claim they will never be brought back to life and especially face judgment.

In verse 14 it ends with a strong statement when they are experiencing the punishment. They are told to 'taste ye your trial'. Next in that same verse the fact that they always asked for this judgment is now being brought up to increase them in their misery. The unbelievers in Mecca used to challenge the Prophet to bring on the punishment because they rejected its truth.

Jesus in the Gospels stressed that the unbelievers loved the glory of man above the glory that comes from God in John 12:43. Their priorities are reversed in that they seek this worldly life whereas they should be seeking the next life and feel comfortable that God will take care of their worldly needs in Matthew 6:32-33. This focus on worldly life and the worldly glories of men cause them to gauge their actions on worldly results and neglect the punishment in the Hereafter.

5.1.4. Facts about Disbelief and Disbelievers

On the subject of disbelief and disbelievers this section is the largest. There are more explanations of what constitutes disbelief than any other types in this chapter. There are many topics covered such as the feelings toward the Prophets and the causes of destruction for those who do not believe in them and their messages. These verses are hard to categorize so there are many verses that form their own category.

The transition from one category to another may appear haphazard given the diversity of these verses.

Disobey and Feel Safe

One of the temptations away from faith by the Devil is the quaint idea that so long as their mischief goes unnoticed or worse it is accepted in society that there will be no account for their crimes. In Chapter 7 verse 99 a question is asked if those who disobey God actually feel secure from the Plan of God. Ibn Kathir explained this verse with a dichotomy. A believer worships through fear and anxiety because they know how powerful God is and how He can do anything at any time. An unbeliever disobeys God as he feels he is safe from Him all the time.

In the Gospels, belief is central to being saved from the wrath of God. In John 3:36 it is stated that those who believe in Jesus will have everlasting life, i.e. go to Heaven, while those who do not will receive the wrath of God, i.e. go to Hell. These are stark words of warning which are only heeded by those who fear God and do not feel safe from His wrath. It might be the same situation in which babies who do not know any better approach danger without fear, except this ignorance in life is not accepted by God just as a baby grows older and gradually begins to learn about dangers in this life to his/her benefit.

Those Who Hate the Prophets Will Be Forgotten

Chapter 108 according to Ibn Kathir was revealed because one of the enemies of Muhammad named As b. Wa'il used to scorn him. As b. Wa'il used to say that the Prophet would eventually be forgotten because he did not have any descendants (no children) with his first wife, Khadija. In verse 3 this claim is refuted and reversed on the unbelievers. It is the unbelievers who will be forgotten as stated previously.

The hatred towards Muhammad was similar to the hatred shown Jesus. In the Gospels Jesus pointed out in John 7:7 that the world hated him because he showed that the works of the unbelievers within it were evil. The truth is always hardest to hear especially when this truth is at the core of people's beliefs and behaviors. Muhammad and

Jesus did not shy away from pointing out the evil of the world whatever it was and because of that they were hated in their time and even
today.

Muhammad Rejected Like Those Before Him

The hatred shown to Muhammad from the people of Mecca was not
unlike the hatred shown to other Prophets in other places. The Qur'an
recounts many of these stories some of which are found in the Bible,
too. Some stories are only found in the Qur'an. In Chapter 35 verse 4
Muhammad is linked to these other Prophets and their vicissitudes. In
this verse it is indicated that Muhammad was rejected by the unbelievers like the Messengers before his time.

This concept is repeated in Chapter 29 verse 18 which indicates
that the nations before the Meccans had rejected their Messengers
also. Ibn Kathir explained that the ruins of these nations can be
found all around, which are proof of the results of disbelief. Further,
this verse emphasizes that the eventual fate of disbelievers and their
nations are not the concern of the Prophet. All he has to do is convey the message.

The rejection of the people of Mecca still distressed Muhammad
despite this reality. Chapter 6 verses 33 to 34 comfort him regarding
this rejection. In this consolation it is stated that the people are not
rejecting him, but they reject the revelation. The Prophet was and
remained a respected man in Mecca and abroad for his fair-dealing and
trustworthiness.

In verse 34 the topic of the Prophets being abused and denied
before Muhammad is repeated. This verse stresses the need to be
patient and constant until God delivers His aid. Change is not easy
or quick.

Amongst the tribes of Israel when Jesus came their rejection of him
was consistent with their rejection of former Prophets. Jesus was told
in Matthew 5:12 that he should be happy because he will get a great
reward in Heaven. He was rejected and persecuted just like the Prophets that came before him. This consolation is also in the Qur'an directed at the Prophet Muhammad.

People Swear Their Support to Any Prophet

Ibn Kathir explained that the Arabs and in particular the Meccans committed themselves to following the Messenger when or if he came to them. This is brought up in Chapter 35 verse 42. They thought that they would be more supportive of this future Prophet than other nations.

This verse explains that despite these commitments when the Prophet declared himself as such they rejected him and increased in their disbelief. The Arabs in this regard, despite their insistence to be otherwise, were like everyone else in their treatment of the Prophets and the message. The Prophets instead of bringing a message that was meant to help them achieve salvation end up causing their doom.

This irony is also highlighted in the Gospels in Luke 11:47 when Jesus invoked woe upon those that build monuments to former Prophets who their forefathers had killed. People always assume that they will do the right thing or believe in the right thing, but human nature along with an added push from the greatest enemy, the Devil, causes people to behave in such a way that they oppose those they said they would follow and do things they said they would never do without even realizing it. The tribes of Israel and the Arab tribes were no different in this regard.

Signs Destroy People

In Islam signs can be physical signs such as miracles and non-physical signs such as the verses of the Qur'an. Either way the purpose of the signs is to guide people to God. In Chapter 17 verse 59 the signs referred to are the physical signs. Ibn Kathir explained that the people of Mecca asked the Prophet for proof that he is telling the truth by turning al-Safa (a hill around Mecca) into gold. These people were warned in this verse because if this sign was delivered and the people still did not believe God it would bring destruction upon them. The example of Thamud, the people of Prophet Salih, and the she-camel is given, which will be discussed later.

It is known that these demands for signs are not really tools for those who challenge faith to believe in God or the Messenger. Even if these signs are shown they will still dismiss them as an illusion or some other accusation. Their ultimate objective in demanding these signs is to weaken the message.

It is a sign of strong disbelief that even visual affirmations do not inspire faith. There are several instances in the Meccan verses where this type of disbelief is evident amongst the unbelievers. The Meccans always bothered the Prophet with demands for a miracle. There are reports of many miracles that were performed by Muhammad like Jesus. In these verses it is made clear that these miracles and other visual proofs do not benefit people couched in unfaith.

In Chapter 6 verse 111 the visualizations of the angels and the speaking dead would not move them to faith if shown to them. Further, in Chapter 15 verses 14 to 15 the Gate of Heaven could be shown to them and they would attribute that sight to magic. In both of these accounts amazing things could be shown with little effect on the faith of those who reject it. The splitting of the moon mentioned in Chapter 54 verses 1 to 2 is one example in the Meccan verses where a miracle was done before the eyes of those who do not benefit from faith and they dismissed it as magic. In the Gospels, the people who approached Jesus for miracles did not benefit from their intrinsic meaning in which God is great and they should worship Him and Him alone.

In Chapter 52 verse 44 this inability to accurately gain from the lessons of faith from visual signs also spells their doom. As Ibn Kathir explained regarding this verse, the unbelievers misinterpret their impending doom as something else, something friendlier. This punishment may originate in the atmosphere which they will think are only clouds forming. They resist believing that this is their punishment until it is obvious at the very end.

The demand for signs also occurred during the time of Jesus. The Pharisees approached Jesus in Mark 8:11-12. They asked him for signs as proof that he is a Prophet. Their requests only drew the ire of Jesus and a denial that signs would be shown to that generation because he knew that even if he were to perform these signs for them they would only increase in disbelief. This seems counter-intuitive, but it reveals the true nature of disbelief.

Reject and Oppose the Truth

The response of the unbelievers is also described in Chapter 84 verses 21 to 22. It is noted in these verses that when the Qur'an is read to them they are not inspired to faith in God nor do they bow to His will. Ibn Kathir raised these questions: why don't they believe in God and why don't they prostrate themselves in His Grandeur? The reason for this and the answer to Ibn Kathir's questions is that they do not fear or believe in celestial judgment.

The unbelievers opposed the truth so starkly that they plotted to kill the Messenger who brought it. The Meccans plotted to kill Muhammad before he made his migration to Medina and the Pharisees plotted to kill Jesus. In Matthew 12:14 they held a council to deliberate over how they would destroy Jesus. In Mark 3:6 the Pharisees took council with the Herodians, the ruling elite of Palestine at the time, to determine how they would destroy Jesus. These reactions appear so strange to people later in life. Many Christians living today do not understand the terrible hatred the Pharisees had for Jesus, as Muslims today do not understand the hatred the Meccans had for Muhammad.

Verses of Qur'an Not from the Devil

Many reject the revelations in the Qur'an because of the same vanities that cause them to deny the possibility of there being a Day of Judgment. One of the accusations that has been asserted by modern writers as it was at the time of the Prophet is that the verses of the Qur'an owe their origin with the Devil. In Chapter 26 verses 221 to 224 there is a refutation that the verses of the Qur'an are from the Devil. In contrast, the Qur'an is not wanted by the Devil and his allies.

In these verses it is told that the evil ones descend on those people who are like them, i.e. liars and wicked people. Ibn Kathir singled out fortune-tellers in his explanation which may be indicated in verse 223. Also the poets of whom this chapter is named after are singled out as well. The poets used to recite well-versed poetry and gain fame in Arabia. Some of them turned their talents against the Prophet and Islam. Muhammad also used to be accused of only being a skilled poet of which he had no training nor did he ever recite poetry before the verses of the Qur'an.

The accusation that the verses of the Qur'an are of the Devil is something that gained notoriety in the 1980s with Salman Rushdie's fictional retelling of a story found in some traditions where Satan causes some foul verses that attribute partners in worship with God to be inserted into the Qur'an. According to the tradition, God causes these verses to be removed because of their source. This story is found in the accounts of al-Tabari who received the account from Ibn Sa'd who received the account from al-Waqidi. The account is not found in the trustworthy accounts in Bukhari or Muslim and the tradition or *hadith* is largely considered to be *da'if* (weak) which means that its chain of narrators (*isnad*) has problems of some sort or another.[50] Despite the fact that these stories are a fabrication today this account is taken as a factual retelling by those who seek to discredit the Prophet and the Qur'an not unlike those who made similar accusations at the time of the Prophet and at the time of Jesus.

The Pharisees used to claim that Jesus got his power to exorcise demons from the possessed from the Devil. This claim is made in Matthew 9:34. It is made again in Matthew 12:24. Jesus responded to this accusation in Matthew 12:25 by stating an analogy that a kingdom that is divided is destroyed which indicates that Jesus did not serve two masters, i.e. God and the Devil. He served God alone and he exorcised possessed people through His Power alone. The Devil is and always will be the enemy of those who believe and is not an ally of any Prophet through the ages despite the derogatory accounts claiming an alliance.

5.2. The Issue of Disbelief: The Qur'an

In the Qur'an there are several verses that do not have counter-parts in the Gospels, but are significant verses for understanding the Islamic perspective on disbelief. Some of these sections are the same as in the

---

[50] Saifullah, M. M., Iqbal, Q., Ahmed, M., & Ghoniem, M. (1999, August 23). *«Those Are The High Flying Claims»*. Retrieved August 8, 2014, from www.islamic-awareness.org/Polemics/sverses.html.

previous section, but the sub-sections are different. There are also some new sections that are not in the previous section.

5.2.1. Earthly Results of Disbelief

The deeds of the unbelievers, though on the surface appear great, are actually not benefiting them in the eyes of God. The real benefits are from the revelations which do not reach the hearts of these people so they do not benefit from them as discussed in the previous section. Their continued transgressions lead to added restrictions from God and punishments which only cause them to go more astray. They despair at these punishments which really are only the lighter forms of punishment because the great punishment is the punishment of the Hereafter, i.e. Hell. These concepts are addressed in this section.

The Deeds Add to Nothing

Those who reject the signs/verses of God and the Hereafter are specifically mentioned in this verse in Chapter 7 verse 147. Those who reject the signs of God as well as His Hereafter are essentially unbelievers.

In this verse it is stated that their deeds do not add up to anything. In this case the deeds are those that are honorable by Islamic standards, but mean nothing if someone does not have the proper faith. This shows the centrality of faith in Islamic doctrine.

In the case of this verse the idea of getting what one works for is emphasized. People do good things for different reasons. In Islam the doing of good deeds should be done for God and God alone. If someone does good things because they want other people to see them, then this is rejected by God.

Added Restrictions for Those Who Disobey

Those who received added restrictions due to their disobedience refer to those who had received messages from God, but then disobeyed them after accepting them. In Chapter 6 verse 146 the very restrictive dietary laws of some communities of the *Ahl al-Kitab* (People of the Book) are referenced. These dietary laws are not imposed upon the Muslims because they were imposed on these former communities for their disobedience.

Ibn Kathir explained that these dietary restrictions were the result of rebellion and defying the commandments of God. It can be assumed that prior commands were not as restrictive, but due to negligence these were increased. There are other verses of the Qur'an that mention some dietary restrictions that were invented by men and were not commands of God. These are not referenced in this verse.

The Lighter Torment Is First

In Chapter 32 verse 21 it is stated that the punishment of the Hereafter is experienced in a lesser version in this life. This appears counter to the verses described previously that note that disbelief is rewarded with the good things of this life such as wealth. It cannot be ignored that even people who have everything still experience calamity such as disease and other problems in this world. Ibn Kathir explained that these calamities are the lighter torments before the heavier torments in the Hereafter which are more severe.

In Islam all things are a test including wealth and hardship. In essence the lighter torment may provide a reminder to those sailing down the wrong path that they will be held accountable for their crimes in the form of punishment which is Hell. There are many people who have experienced a traumatic event that afterward caused them to be more faithful and remember God more. This may be the reason for these calamities. Those who do not learn from these experiences will then experience the greater torment, i.e. Hell. Since no one has experienced Hell and have come back to talk about it we can only compare it with the torments in this world which by our estimation are great.

5.2.2. Hereafter Results of Disbelief

One of the points that are added to the previous section on this issue is the issue of regret on behalf of those who did not believe when they face judgment at the end of time. The end result of their life on earth will be external and internal misery. The other point in this section is the reality that those in Hell will expect certain people to be there, but they will not find them because they are in Heaven. This shows the twisted nature of these people that they perceived those who were good in this life as bad.

Regrets

The regret of those who did not obey God in this life in the Hereafter is captured in Chapter 15 verse 2 which states that the people of Hell will wish they were Muslims. Ibn Kathir explained that this specifically pertains to the time when unbelievers and sinful Muslims will be in Hell together. According to Islamic belief one day these sinful Muslims will be rescued from Hell because at their core they still recognized the Oneness of God. At that time the unbelievers, or those who did not recognize the Oneness of God, will wish they had been Muslims in their earthly life.

This regret extends beyond core theological issues, but into actions they did or did not do in this life. In Islam, the Hereafter is the ultimate justice. Murderers, rapists, spendthrifts, misers and all sorts of unseemly people may elude justice in this life, but they will not escape it in the Hereafter. In Chapter 74 verses 43 to 44 those who are in Hell will admit that they deserved this fate and will begin listing reasons why. In the case of these verses they will admit that they did not worship God and/or do good to other people.

This regret regarding belief and actions leads to a final proclamation that juxtaposes this regret to their lack of regret to living the high life on the Earth. In Chapter 89 verse 24 the person of Hell will exclaim that s/he did not send any good deeds ahead for his/her next life in grief. Good deeds are the provisions of the Hereafter like money in this life. Men scramble for more money, but this is short term. Men should be scrambling for the good deeds. How different would this Earth look if this was the case?

Further, as Ibn Kathir explained for this verse, beyond the disobedient feeling sorry for not obeying God, the righteous in this life will also feel regret because they were unable to send more good deeds forward to the Hereafter. This is a profound statement since many who worship God rigorously these days feel they are above everyone else. This statement indicates that no one should be satisfied with the good they do because it is never enough to assuage the fears one will experience on Judgment Day.

People of Hell Will Look for Others

In Hell as described in the Qur'an there will be a lot of accusations and soul-searching over how they got there. As noted previously they will admit to what got them there. In Chapter 38 verses 62 to 63 the people of Hell will look around for those people they thought misguided while they thought that they were believers. Their ultimate frustration in Hell will be realized when they will not find these people because they are in Heaven.

This section on the Hereafter results of disbelief has shown contrasts with the earthly results. People appear quite successful in this life and it appears like their way is the best way. They will even deceive themselves. These verses here show how much they had deceived themselves because their views were so distorted that good people who went to Heaven appeared to them in this life to be evil people.

5.2.3. Stubbornness of the Unbelievers

This section highlights some of the verses in the Meccan period that focus on the stubbornness of those who reject faith in the One God. This stubbornness has prevented many people from accepting the messages of Jesus and Muhammad. In this section this stubbornness is reflected in their demands for another message besides the one brought by Muhammad.

Demand another Message

In Chapter 10 verse 15 the unbelievers absurdly demand another message. Most of the time that trouble comes to the Prophets whether it is in the Qur'an or the Bible is because they brought messages that offended some segment of the population that was powerful. Jesus offended the Pharisees and Muhammad offended the Meccans. When Islam started to be preached publicly after the first three years challenging the religious sentiments of the predominant religion they insulted and oppressed the Muslims, negotiated with the Prophet and discredited him amongst other things.

In this verse the unbelievers want the message that Muhammad brought to be changed to match their desires and beliefs. The answer is that it is not his message to change and if he did he would be in trouble with God. Messages are meant to challenge these beliefs because the cause for the message was error in belief. By their nature the Prophets were and are controversial to this day.

5.2.4. Criticism of God Bearing Children

There are several verses in the Meccan period that refute and challenge the idea that God has children. The initial thought is that this is a rejection of the Christian Trinitarian thought, which it is, but the pagan Arabs also believed that God had children. Some of these verses are directed specifically at the pagan Arabs. These verses can be categorized under two concepts which are general rejections of the idea and warnings for believing in this theology.

General Rejection of God Having Children

Chapter 19 verses 88 to 92 contain some of the strongest rejections of God having children in the whole Qur'an. The accusation that God has children causes the skies to burst, the earth to split and the mountains to fall down (90). Ibn Kathir explained that these things occur because of the anger of God at these statements.

Beside these strong rejections, Muhammad is told to tell those who say such things that if it were true he would worship this son. It is obvious that this concept is rejected since he never ascribed a son to God let alone worshipped him. Chapter 43 verse 81 contains this recommended refutation of this idea as well as Chapter 39 verse 4 which points out the ignorance in these claims.

Warnings for Believing God Has Children

On top of rejecting this concept is a warning for believing in it. In Chapter 10 verse 68 the idea of God having children is rejected again, but in addition to this rejection is the claim that those who say this have no warrant for this. The verse questions why they say things about God that they do not know. Ibn Kathir explained that this is an admonition for believing in this concept.

In Chapter 18 verse 4 those who ascribe a son to God are addressed in particular for that warning. In verse 2 of this chapter it states that this revelation was sent to warn those in error and reinforce the righteous. Those who associate children with God are therefore warned in verse 4. Ibn Kathir explained that this verse is addressed to the pagan Arabs who worshipped the angels as daughters of God.

5.2.5. Facts about Disbelief and Disbelievers

There are many topics covered in this sub-section such as the influence of the devil and the feelings of the unbelievers. Similarly to the previous section on the same topic these verses are hard to categorize so the transition from one set of verses to the next does not flow as well as in other sections. These verses, as before, also are the largest collection of verses in this section.

Disbelievers Despair

The believer is expected to accept calamities as a test from God and 'roll with the punches.' In contrast, the disbeliever cannot accept calamities and they complain until the event has ended and their life has been restored to normal. This contrast is established in this section.

In Chapter 10 verse 12, the distressed person cries out, but when all is okay this same person acts arrogant and turns away from God who causes the distress to leave the person. This same situation is repeated in Chapter 11 verses 9 to 10. In those verses the person without faith despairs when bad things happen to them, but becomes ecstatic when blessings come their way. In a way, the manner that one behaves when faced with adversity determines whether s/he is a believer or not.

A similar situation can be found in Chapter 29 verse 10. In this verse the tests imposed on the nascent Muslim community have caused some to exit Islam. This is addressed here by noting that faith is only on their lips which they speak of only when there is a victory. This is not the behavior of the faithful who endure through good times and bad times while retaining their faith and not giving into despair.

Most People Are Misguided

When people despair over calamities they are showing signs of disbelief, but in the Meccan verses one verse clearly explains that most people on the Earth are astray. In Chapter 6 verse 116 there is a warning for those who have faith. As explained by Ibn Kathir this verse indicates that most people on Earth are misguided so do not follow them otherwise their path will become their own. It is stressed by Ibn Kathir that a believing Muslim should only obey the Prophet Muhammad.

God Guides and Leads Astray

The fact that most people are misguided is followed in the same chapter by the idea that only God guides. In Chapter 6 verse 125 it is stated that God guides who He wills and leaves astray those He wills. For those left astray their hearts are closed to faith as Ibn Kathir explained. Their hearts are so closed that it is impassable and the verse uses the analogy of the breast being so tight that it is like one who has to climb up to the sky. Ibn Kathir added that it is the weight of faith that causes this constriction. This is the same concept of those who do not benefit from the Qur'an as mentioned previously.

The Influence of the Devil

One of the major reasons why people go astray both in Islam and in Christianity is because of the allure of the Devil. There will be an interesting speech given by the Devil in the future after Judgment Day when all those destined for Hell are collected there. In Chapter 14 verse 22 the Devil disowns his followers. He basically confides in them that he was in error and he sought to make them in error. They look to him as their leader and in this time he will disassociate himself from them. This will be a miserable time for them, but they were warned.

This situation is further explained in Chapter 19 verse 83 in that the Devil and his aides are sent to the unbelievers to push them to do evil.

In Islam, belief is the only shield against this onslaught which when absent opens one's heart to the influences of these evil ones. These people are urged to hate those who believe according to Ibn Kathir. When one sees all the violence against Muslim and Christian communities around the globe this verse and its explanation ring true on many levels.

Try to Weaken Revelation

Disobedience causes people to reject the Word of God. The people have continued this long tradition of man from the time of Adam all the way to the time of Muhammad. In all ages including this one it is always a reality. Revelation stands to oppose those practices and false beliefs, so those who do not believe in them work hard to rub them down or weaken their impact.

In Chapter 18 verse 56 it is made clear that the Messengers are sent solely to give good news for those who believe and warnings for those who do not believe. The unbelievers strive to weaken this message and actually mock it. In both stories of Jesus and Muhammad they were surrounded by people who mocked them and their message, but today those who mocked are now forgotten while those who they mocked will be remembered forever.

Deny Judgment Day

In Chapter 74 verse 46 there is one answer in a series of answers to the question in verse 42: What led you into hellfire? In verse 46 they (the people of Hell) will say that in their life they denied the Day of Judgment. The verse that immediately precedes that (45) indicates that they used to talk vanities.

One of these vanities is the doubt they cast on the possibility of there being a resurrection for judgment. In Chapter 79 verses 27 to 28 there is an answer to the doubts the unbelievers have regarding the resurrection. It is asked whether it is harder to create people (or recreate them after death) or to create the heavens.

The mistake in thinking there will be no judgment for their sins in this life will become more poignant when the event actually occurs. In Chapter 79 verse 46 it is asserted that when the Day of Judgment occurs it will feel as if this life was so short that it was only an afternoon of one day. At times this life feels like it is long, but it is often heard that life is a blur. Childhood, adult-life and elderly-life can seemingly occur in a blink of an eye. Death is never too far away from any of us and the impending judgment should not be thought of as so far off that it may never happen to them.

Seek Compromise in Disbelief

At some point in Mecca, as indicated in the story of Islam in Mecca previously, the Meccan leaders attempted to negotiate with the Prophet. The community was becoming divided over Islam and the leadership was hopeful that peace could be achieved and everyone could get what they want. The Prophets throughout history never negotiated on matters of faith. Jesus did not negotiate with his opponents and neither did Muhammad. After all this was the purpose of them delivering their message in the first place.

The rejection of compromise with disbelief is codified in Chapter 109 in which faith and unfaith are clearly separated. Ibn Kathir explained that the people of Mecca invited the Prophet to worship their gods for a year in exchange for them worshipping the God of Muhammad for a year. This is rejected in this chapter.

Chapter 109 states, "(1) Say: O you that reject Faith! (2) I do not worship that which you worship, (3) Nor will you worship that which I worship. (4) And I will not worship that which you have been wont to worship, (5) Nor will you worship that which I worship. (6) To you be your Way, and to me mine."[51]

Their Desires Corrupt Heaven and Earth

The desires of the unbelievers to have a syncretistic religion that would combine polytheism and monotheism ends up corrupting the message and purpose of the Prophets coming in the first place. In Chapter 23 verse 71 the desires of the unbelievers are addressed. It is noted that if

---

[51] Ali, A. Y. (2010). *The Meaning of the Glorious Qur'an*. Istanbul, Turkey: ASIR Media. (p. 422).

God followed their desires the Heaven and the Earth would be corrupted. Ibn Kathir explained that mankind is both incapable and
inconsistent in their ideas and desires. This inconsistency is far removed
from the consistency of God and His capabilities.

Admit the Error on their Deathbed

All of the accusations, the vanities and the hope for compromise on
faith and unfaith will not benefit the unbelievers in the Hereafter. Far
from holding onto all these false beliefs the Qur'an asserts that upon
death and the questioning of the angels they will admit that they were
in error. The angels will ask where the people/gods/etc. that they called
on other than God are now and they will respond that they have left
them. With this answer they will admit that they were wrong.

This admission to error can be found in Chapter 7 verses 37 to 39.
Also in these verses is a dialogue between the different generations of
unbelievers. The last generation will blame the first generation for their
disbelief and the first generation will disavow themselves from the later
generations. It is asserted in these verses that they will all have equal
punishment. Being born to unbelievers does not mean one has to be
an unbeliever.

5.3. Summary

The Gospels and the Qur'an both address issues of disbelief because it
was a problem at the time of Jesus as well as the time of Muhammad.
The messages of these two men resonate on some of the earthly and
hereafter results of disbelief as well as outlining the claims of the disbelievers and facts about disbelief. There are additional teachings in the
Qur'an on these subjects which are included in this chapter. These add
more points on the Islamic perspective of disbelief while not conflict-
ing with the message in the Gospel.

Regarding the earthly results of disbelief both the Qur'an and the
Gospel include wealth as being a sign of disbelief while the message in
the Gospels is more sweeping than the message in the Qur'an. In the
Qur'an wealth is not necessarily linked with disbelief while it is in the

Gospels. Despite this slight difference both messages note that those who disbelieve receive no benefits from the messages that Jesus or Muhammad brought to them in which Jesus added that only believers can actually hear his message. These disbelievers not only avoid any benefit these messages bring them, they also are punished by God because they oppressed the Prophets sent to them according to both the Qur'an and the Gospels. Lastly, the disbelievers are highly influenced by the Devil because they do not turn towards God and are lost as described by the messages brought by Muhammad and Jesus.

The Qur'an adds some additional teachings on the earthly results of disbelief in that the deeds of the unbelievers are not recognized by God no matter how good they may appear to be in this life. In addition, those who disobey God are further burdened with additional commands that would not have existed had they followed the original commands of God. The unbelievers may also experience lighter torments in this life before the greater torment of the Hereafter, i.e. Hell.

In the Hereafter results of disbelief both the Qur'an and the Gospels note that while God may have considered everyone in this life, in the next life those who disbelieved in this life will be totally forgotten by God in the fires of Hell without consolation. In addition, in both of these messages those who once believed and then left faith for unfaith will be punished with these fires from Hell which can be seen in the story of Jesus in regards the demise of Judas after he betrayed Jesus. The Qur'an alone adds that those whose eventual end will be Hell will regret that they did not live a life of faith and good works while those in Hell will look for those they expected to be in Hell who are actually in Heaven.

In both the Qur'an and the Gospels it addresses the claims by those who state that Jesus and Muhammad invented the message or were in league with the Devil. Both of these Messengers responded that the revelations are from God alone. It is clear in both the Qur'an and the Gospel that God gave the message to them without consideration of their worldly status and they were only men because they ate and slept like all men. Lastly, the unbelievers believe that they will never be held accountable for their misdeeds when they die because they are focused on worldly glories in exchange for the glories of the Hereafter.

There are a number of facts about disbelief in both the Gospels and the Qur'an. In both messages it is stated that no one is safe from the eventual judgment from God in that only proper faith will save people from Hell. Those who do not have the proper faith are those who hate the Prophets because they point out the evil in this world, but these people will eventually be forgotten. In this life the unbelievers may think they are doing the right thing, but often times they do the wrong thing. They are so misled that they even think the messages from the Prophets are from the Devil which is refuted in both the Qur'an and the Gospels. They remain obstinate in their disbelief no matter what is shown them and oppose the message to the point that they plot to kill the Prophets. Despite the hatred towards these Prophets, the Prophets are eventually rewarded greatly in the end.

The Qur'an alone adds that the disbelievers despair when ill reaches them, but rejoice when good things happen to them. These people are misguided in that only God guides whom He wills while most people in this world are misguided. Those who are misguided work to rub down the message brought by the Messengers and deny the Day of Judgment, the Devil is working rigorously to misguide people, such as encouraging them to mix faith and unfaith and make their desires their focus. Sadly, on their deathbed they will admit their error which will be too late for repentance.

The Qur'an alone also adds that the unbelievers are very stubborn in their disbelief in that they demand another message other than the one brought to them by the Prophet sent to them. The disbelievers are also called out in the Qur'an for attributing children to God in which the Qur'an clearly states that God does not have any children. The Arabs who believed the angels were the daughters of God are warned about harboring this belief in the Qur'an.

Chapter 6

The Commands

The Commands

I n the first three years there were some commands such as to worship the One God and pray. The remaining ten years had many
more commands than the first three in Mecca. The Medinan era
had many more commands than the Meccan era mostly because the
Muslim community had more freedom and responsibility there than
they did in Mecca.

Many critics claim that the Medinan era abrogated the Meccan era.
They especially use this concept to brush away all the commands in
Mecca to forgive those who attack and offend you by pointing out the
permission to fight the enemies of Islam given in Medina. This is not
to say that abrogation did not happen. The topic is addressed in the
Qur'an in a Meccan chapter (16:101) and a Medinan chapter (2:106).
The determination of which verses were abrogated by later verses is a
topic of scholarly contention of which most are especially internet lay-
men who are not well-versed and are more interested in spreading hate
towards Islam and Muslims than actually getting the facts. The most
common accepted example is the gradual curtailment of alcohol consumption which was finally forbidden absolutely in Medina. The sub-
stitution for war over peace in some contexts is not as simple as saying
Muhammad had a change of mind that has forever locked the Muslim
people into militancy. This topic is addressed later in this book.

In Mecca there were various commands such as showing forgiveness,
inviting to Islam, being kind to one's parents, being fair and just, and
fulfilling one's promises. Each of these commands are addressed separately. In essence it may be this chapter that is the most interesting to
the reader. Religion is belief and action. The previous chapter captured
the dichotomy between faith and unfaith in the teachings of Muhammad
and Jesus. This chapter moves a step forward to actions as embodied by

commands. The topic of proper faith also appears in these commands such as the command to reject polytheism and believe in God alone. There are several verses in the Meccan period that forbid or encourage multiple behaviors and beliefs in one verse. These verses will be cited multiple times to cover these different aspects in separate sections. These verses are 6:151, 7:33, 17:23, 25:68, and 30:31.

6.1. The Commands: The Qur'an and the Gospels

6.1.1. Be Respectful and Show Forgiveness

There are several perspectives on being respectful and showing forgiveness towards those who do not believe in Islam. There are clear verses in the Meccan period that inform the believers to forgive those who do not believe and harm the Muslim community. On top of this forgiveness are verses that enjoin the Muslims to seek peace with them. Further, with the goal of peace in mind, the Muslims are encouraged to be patient with the wrongs that they experience because they are Muslim. Lastly, the believers are told to leave the non-Muslims alone and not to disrespect their deities while they are still enjoined to remind them of the error of their ways. These separate injunctions are discussed in the following sections.

Forgive

In Chapter 15 verse 85 it is first declared that God created the Heavens and Earth to manifest the truth according to Ibn Kathir's interpretation. In this regard the creation serves as a reminder to mankind that God is his/her Lord in which He has all power to both create and destroy. The reference to destruction comes immediately after this when the issue of the 'Hour' is mentioned. The 'Hour' refers to Judgment Day. After these points are made those who accept this message are instructed to forgive/ overlook the faults of those who do not believe in this message.

Chapter 7 verse 199 similarly and clearly instructs the Muslims to forgive/show forgiveness while avoiding the ignorant. The ignorant are not only those who disbelieve, but those who disbelieve and actively encourage others to disbelieve. On top of this the verse commands the Muslims to speak for justice. The topic of upholding justice is addressed later in this chapter.

A very strong exhortation to forgive is made in Chapter 45 verse 14 in which the Prophet was taught to tell the Muslims to forgive the unbelievers. In this verse God is clearly the final judge over who is on the path that is straight. Ibn Kathir explained this verse that the believers should forgive the unbelievers in which this action will secure the unbelievers punishment in the Hereafter or cause them to reconsider their faithlessness and move towards Islam. Either way, the eventual end is not up to the Muslims.

The topic of forgiveness is not only directed from Muslims to non-Muslims, but amongst themselves. This includes crimes that merit capital punishment in Islam. In Chapter 42 verse 40 the idea of an eye for an eye (equal recompense) is made permissible in Islam, but forgiveness is considered a better option. According to Ibn Kathir's explanation of this verse, equal justice (*qisas*) is allowed, but forgiveness is recommended. Ibn Kathir further explained that this increases the person who forgives in honor before God.

Forgiving someone who harms someone is not easy. In Chapter 42 verse 43, only 3 verses later from the previous verse, the word patience is used along with forgiveness. This verse explains that those who forgive are courageous and resolute. Ibn Kathir explained that bearing the insult with patience and further even concealing the evil action is recommended in which this action will entitle the forgiving person to a great reward from God.

Being patient is considered one of the items on the path that is steep. In Chapter 90 verses 11 to 17 the path that is steep is explained. It is described as a direction that is hard to achieve, but not impossible. In verse 17 one of the qualities of this steep path is being patient with the harms of the people while being merciful. In verse 18 that follows this the people that can do this will be 'Companions of the Right Hand' which are those people destined for Heaven.

Along the lines of being patient is also seeking peace. In Chapter 25 verse 63 the behaviors of the Muslims are described in ideal. They walk with dignity and humility, not with arrogance. When the ignorant address them their response should not only be to forgive, but to seek peace with them. In this case they are instructed to say the word 'peace' to them.

The exhortation to seek peace with the ignorant is restated in Chapter 43 verse 89. Ibn Kathir explained that the Muslims are told not to respond in like manner to those that address them rudely. They are told to turn away (ignore them) and offer them something better in word and deed.

In line with ignoring them there are verses in the Meccan period that inform the Muslims to leave them alone and give them respite. In Chapter 6 verse 70 the Muslims are told to ignore those who take religion as a joke and for play because one day they will be judged by God for these beliefs and actions. This is repeated in Chapter 43 verse 83. While the Muslims are told to ignore them they are not exempted from reminding them of their potential recompense for their ill behavior.

In Chapter 86 verses 15 and 17 the plotting of those who hate Islam is given as an example. They plot, but so does God. The Muslims are told to wait regarding these people because one day they will be judged according to their words and actions.

Throughout all of these verses the issue of forgiveness, patience and giving respite permeated them all. Muslims are expected to do and say only those things that are good no matter what other people do to or say to them. This exhortation is repeated in Chapter 17 verse 53 in which the Muslims are instructed to say only those things that are considered the best because the Devil uses ill-words to cause divisions amongst people. Further in Chapter 23 verse 96 the Muslims are again told to repel evil with those things that are better than it; i.e. do not respond to evil words and actions with similar evil words and actions. As explained by Ibn Kathir, treat kindly those that treat others badly in order to soften their heart and create bonds of friendship. Ibn Kathir added that only the very patient people are really able to do this.

There is a trap for the Muslim that responding to their insults will lower them to their level. In Chapter 6 verse 108 the Muslims are told not to insult their false deities because they respond with more insults of the One God. Again this verse points out that their words and deeds will be compensated for in the Hereafter. There is no need to insult them or their deities especially since Muslims should enjoin the good and forbid the evil.

Forgiving those who hurt others and say hurtful things is also a major theme in the teachings of Jesus in the Gospels. In Mark 11:25 the believers are told that when they are praying they should forgive those that have wronged them so that God may forgive the supplicant. The disciples were taught a prayer which is known as the Lord's Prayer in Christianity which stresses forgiveness. In Matthew 6:12 the prayer asks for forgiveness for their debts as they are to forgive the debts of others. In Matthew 6:14 the prayer asks for the forgiveness of their trespasses as they forgive others that trespass against them.

The issue of forgiveness merits a story in the teachings of Jesus about a King who forgave the debt of one of his servants in Matthew 18:23-35. In the story the King forgave the debt of this servant who then went out and demanded the debt from one of his debtors. When the debtor could not pay the debt he had him thrown in prison. When the King learnt of his lack of forgiveness that had been shown him the King recalled the servant to his court and confronted him about his lack of compassion. The King then had him tortured till he could pay his debt. In verse 35 Jesus explained that this is an analogy of the forgiveness sought after by mankind from God. If they desire forgiveness then they should learn to forgive others as well.

The teachings of Jesus also extend beyond forgiving to bearing patiently with the wrongs of others as it is in the Qur'an. In Matthew 5:38-42 the concept of retribution is rejected in which the believers are told when they are struck they are to turn the other cheek to be struck as well (39), if they are sued they are to give the person who sues them double what he has asked for (40), if they are forced to walk a mile, they are to walk two (41) and if they are asked they are instructed to give (42). Later in verse 44 they are told to love their enemies and do good to them. This is the same instructions in the Qur'an regarding the doing of good in response to evil being done to them.

6.1.2. Missionizing

Even though the Muslims are exhorted to leave those who do not believe alone, this does not exempt them from the injunction to spread the word of Islam. There are a number of verses during the Meccan period that instruct the Muslims to invite people to Islam. These verses command the Muslims to invite in a good manner with good speech and not by force. The idea that Islam is a religion spread by the sword or through force is not supported in the Qur'an. It can easily be argued that it is not supported by history either which is a theme that has been covered in other books.

The concept of inviting others to the faith is also covered in the Gospels. In Matthew 10:5-6, Jesus instructed his 12 disciples to preach to the people of Israel that were lost, but not to the Gentiles or to the Samaritans, which was considered a heretical Jewish group. This is interesting because later in Christianity under the stewardship of Paul it became incumbent to preach to the Gentiles (non-Jews) but it was taught through a dichotomy between 'justification by faith' versus 'justification by works.' The Gentiles were expected to have faith through Jesus as means to save them from Hell, but they were not expected to embrace Jewish law which was for the Jews only.[52] This seems counter to the message of Jesus in which he instructed in Matthew 5:17-20 that he came to fulfill the Law in which those who break the Law or teach others to break it will be the 'least in the kingdom of heaven.' Later in verse 20, Jesus praised the Pharisees, who in other places he castigates, as being righteous and that no one would enter Heaven unless their righteousness exceeded those people.

The concept that Jesus was sent only to the People of Israel would help solve this conflict in Christianity because Jesus confirmed the Law which is for the Jews only. He preached about crucial issues of faith not embraced by the Jews at that time such as eternal life, the resurrection of the body, the reward and punishment in the Hereafter and the

---

[52] Eisenbaum, P. (2010). *Paul Was Not a Christian: The Original Message of a Misunderstood Apostle.* New York, NY: HarperOne.

inner meanings of the Law, i.e. the faith that is supposed to propel its practice.[53] These are concepts that are united in Islam.

There is one story in the Gospels that Jesus was preaching to the People of Israel only. In Matthew 15:22-26, a Canaanite woman came to Jesus asking for help because her daughter was possessed with a demon. Jesus ignored her and explained to his disciples that he was only sent to the 'lost sheep of the house of Israel.' The woman persisted in which Jesus responded through a metaphor that he was not to take the children's bread (his teachings/miracles/good works) and cast it to the dogs (Gentiles).

After the crucifixion and the resurrection the disciples encountered Jesus again who then instructed them in Mark 16:15 to go out into the world and preach the Gospel to all creatures. This is the verse that inspires many Christian missionaries today. Unfortunately, these verses at the end of Mark (the last 12 verses) were added later and are not part of the original manuscript that is the Book of Mark.[54] This is important because Mark is the oldest telling of the story of Jesus.[55] The command to go out and preach the Gospel is made in Matthew 28:19-20 as well.

After the first three years, the public preaching of Islam began in Mecca. There are several verses that encourage this with instructions on how to do this. In Chapter 16 verse 125 it is commanded that when an invitation to Islam is made it should be done with wisdom, kindness, gentleness and the best of speech. There is no room in Islamic manners for rudeness and unkindness in anything that is done, but especially when spreading the word of Islam. The previous section noted that it is not good practice to revile the deities of those who do not believe in Islam. In this verse this type of speech would not be considered acceptable for conveying the message of Islam.

---

[53] Ibid.

[54] Ehrman, B. D. (2007). *Misquoting Jesus: The Story Behind Who Changed the Bible and Why*. New York, NY: HarperSanFrancisco.

[55] Ehrman, B. D. (2009). *Jesus, Interrupted: Revealing the Hidden Contradictions in the Bible (and Why We Don't Know About Them)*. New York, NY: HarperOne.

The People of the Book or the Christians and the Jews are specifically addressed in Chapter 29 verse 46. The Muslims are told in the Qur'an that they are only to argue with them in a good manner. This verse separates those who inflict wrong from this consideration, which is discussed later in this book. Instead the Muslims are given a recommended response to the People of the Book in this verse. This response is one of the central beliefs of Islam. Muslims believe there is only One God for all people and only one religion that has been called by different names throughout the ages, but essentially is the same thing. This is also the underlying assumption behind this book.

In line with this recommended saying is a *hadith* recorded in the *tafsir* of Ibn Kathir on some advice that Muhammad gave to the Muslims when talking to the People of the Book. It is recorded that the Prophet said, "Do not believe in the People of the Book and do not deny them. Say: 'We believe in God and what has been revealed to us and what has been revealed to you. Our God and your God is One, and to Him we have submitted.'"[56] This advice is represented in this verse as well.

The concept of submitting to God is where the word 'Muslim' derives in that a Muslim is 'one who submits to God.' The word 'Islam' derives from the word 'Salam' which means 'Peace.' In contrast to those who attack Muslims who say Islam is not a religion of peace, Islam is a religion of peace, an inner peace achieved through submitting to God in Islam. It is not a religion that tells Muslims to remain peaceful even when people are oppressing and killing them. This subject will be covered later in this book.

In Islam there are no defined classes or castes. A person is not elevated through money or birth. These things exist in the modern Muslim world, but like many things that exist in the Muslim world today it has nothing to do with Islam. Instead, a person is elevated in status through his words and deeds alone.

In Chapter 41 verse 33 a rhetorical question is posed. Who is better than a person who calls to Islam and does good deeds? The expected answer is that there is no one better than this person.

---

[56] Quran Tafsir Ibn Kathir - Home. (2010, March). Retrieved from www.qtafsir.com/.

Ibn Kathir explained that this person 'practices what he preaches.' He calls people to Islam while he also obeys God according to Islam. There is no room in Islam or any religion for hypocrisy. There is nothing that does more damage to general faithfulness than a hypocritical religious leader for existing and potential members of that congregation. This is why those who reject that religion constantly search for hypocrisy in the leadership of that religion. For example, the National Security Agency (NSA) was monitoring, illegally, the internet pornography-viewing habits of Muslim leaders in the United States to discredit them.[57]

Islam is to be spread through good speech and action. In the early years of Islam the words and behaviors of the Muslims became the conveyors of Islam. It is known in Indonesia that only a handful of traders and missionaries from the Middle East spread Islam in the important centers of Indonesian trade. Once the leaders converted to Islam the rest was history. This was true for Christianity in the Roman and Greek world. Most conversion occurs because of worldly reasons either to fit in or gain some benefit. Once Islam gained political dominance in the Middle East this became the case for most. When Constantine converted to Christianity making it the official religion of Rome the rest of the population followed. The earliest converts are always the most sincere and faithful believers in the faith.

In Chapter 50 verse 45 it is made clear that it is never allowed to convert a non-believer by force to Islam. A Muslim's objective is only to warn them of their potential end destination if they reject faith and do not follow the commands of God. This was never abrogated. Instead it was confirmed in Medina in the most famous verse on there being no compulsion in religion in Chapter 2 verse 256.

6.1.3. Belief and Behaviors

As noted in the previous section the only difference between Muslims according to Islam is the level of faith and action. This section outlines

---

57   Usero, A. & Reilly, R.J. (2013, November 26). *"Top-Secret Document Reveals NSA Spied on Porn Habits as Part of Plan to Discredit 'Radicalizers'"*. Retrieved January 23, 2014, from www.huffingtonpost.com/2013/11/26/nsa-porn-muslims_n_4346128.html.

those beliefs and actions/behaviors that were discussed during the Meccan period. The belief discussed in this section is the rejection of all forms of polytheism. The behaviors range from specific behaviors like eating and other daily actions to more general behaviors such as not behaving arrogantly.

Responsible for Own Deeds

The first part of faith is belief while the second part is deeds, or actions motivated by faith. The issue of good deeds is very important in Islam as it is in other faiths as well. The analogy of the scale is used in Islam to weigh good deeds versus bad deeds. Every person is responsible for his/her own deeds which largely determine whether they go to Heaven or Hell.

In Chapter 10 verse 41 the accusations of the unbelievers towards Muhammad of being a liar inspired a response to his accusers. He was instructed to say that their responsibility was only to themselves. They were not responsible for what the Prophet did nor was he responsible for what they did. This verse stresses personal responsibility for one's own deeds, good or bad. This idea is further reinforced in 34:25 in which it is stated that the believers are not responsible for the unbelievers and the unbelievers are not responsible for the believers.

In Chapter 53 verse 38 it states that no one can bear the burden of another. Ibn Kathir explained that every soul will get what it earns, nothing more and nothing less. S/he will be responsible for their own injustices and they cannot heap them on another person. This is why the Christian idea of Jesus dying on the cross for other people's sins is not accepted in Islam. This is discussed later in the book.

The concept of no one being able to bear the burdens of others is repeated in Chapter 35 verse 18. This verse is a more expanded version of the previous verse. In this verse it is stated that it does not matter how closely related people are, their own deeds will belong to them and them alone.

Ibn Kathir explained this verse by stating that on the Day of Resurrection each person will carry his/her own deeds with him/her for judgment. In this life only those who fear God truly and follow His commands will receive this admonition and act upon it. In this case all of the commands that follow require proper faith (belief in the One God) and the fear of God for there to be any benefit for the one who does them.

The idea of personal responsibility for one's deeds is also captured in the Gospels. The Prophet John in Luke 3:8 declared that people are to produce the 'fruits worthy of repentance,' i.e. good deeds/actions and not rely on their status as people of Abraham. The idea that someone is guaranteed Heaven without the necessary faith in God and through their good actions is rejected here and rejected in the Qur'an.

Be Kind to Parents

One of the good deeds in Islam is to be kind to one's parents. In Chapter 6 verse 151 it is stressed that one should be good to his/her parents. This is repeated in Chapter 17 verse 23. In this verse the believer is exhorted to be kind to his/her parents after emphasizing that they should worship God alone. This verse expands on verse 151 in Chapter 6. It explains that a believer should never utter a word of contempt towards his/her parents, but they should treat them honorably at all times.

In Chapter 29 verse 8 the same stress is also made on being kind to one's parents. In this verse the point made in Chapter 17 verse 23 regarding the kindness shown to parents following the commitment to worship God alone is elaborated on. The command to be kind to one's parents implies that one should obey them. In this verse if one's parents are not Muslims then they should obey them in all things except matters of faith. God rewards this person for both being kind to one's parents and being patient with their attempts to push them into idolatry or faithlessness. The first priority is always obeying God while the second priority is the parents.

This priority is established in Chapter 46 in which after stating in verse 13 that there is One God and those that affirm this will have no fear, it is enjoined on the believer to be good to his/her parents in verse 15. In this verse it tells the oft-repeated story of the hardship his/her mother encountered carrying him/her and then weaning them in which the person does not gain full strength and maturity until much later in life. The one who treats his/her parents well is juxtaposed to the one who does not in verses 17 to 18. This person will be among the disbelievers on the Day of Judgment destined for Hell.

Respecting parents is also a part of the Gospels. In Matthew 15:4 it is stated that God has commanded, referring to the Mosaic Law, the believer to honor his/her mother and father. If this person curses his/her mother or father they are to 'die the death' which is referring also to Mosaic Law. This is repeated in Mark 7:10. There are several places in the Torah / Old Testament that lay out the punishment for not honoring one's parents. In Exodus 21:15 it is stated that whoever hits one of his/her parents is condemned to death. Leviticus 20:9 states that whoever curses one of his/her parents is condemned to death. In Deuteronomy 21:21 the method of execution for the rebellious child is stoning.

No Arrogance

Many treat their parents badly because of arrogance. In Islam arrogance is forbidden. In the Meccan verses arrogance is referred to in the way that a person walks. It is emphasized in these verses that one should not be prideful, but act with humility. In Chapter 17 verse 37 the believers are commanded to not strut about with arrogance because they do not have the power to split the earth or be as tall as the mountains. People are not as great as they think they are, so the best behavior is to be humble.

The believers are described as those who walk on the earth in humility in Chapter 25 verse 63. This is repeated in Chapter 31 verse 18 where it is recommended that a believer not walk with insolence on the earth. Instead, s/he should be cheerful and not prideful/arrogant towards others.

In Chapter 32 verse 15 the believers are again described as those who are not prideful. This verse specifically refers to the revelations of the Qur'an. It was a noted practice amongst the enemies of Islam in Mecca that when the verses of the Qur'an were recited they would scoff at them. It is a sign of belief and humility that when the verses of the Qur'an are recited that the person falls down in prostration out of reverence for them.

Arrogance is also a quality frowned upon in the Gospels. Luke 14:11 states that whoever exalts himself will be brought low and whoever humbles himself will be exalted. This is a powerful statement which probably refers to the Hereafter when punishment is given to the rebellious on this earth and high status is given to the obedient and humble. Another group of verses draws an interesting analogy in Matthew 18:3-4. In these verses the believers are commanded to humble themselves as a little child in order to enter Heaven. In this teaching humbleness is a quality worthy of entry into Heaven which is a very powerful indication of its importance in both Christianity and Islam.

Eating

A part of being humble is recognizing the blessings of God and in particular the blessing of food. The Muslim is supposed to eat only those things over which the Name of God is mentioned. In Chapter 6 verse 118 this command is codified. The verse that immediately follows this command makes an exception for those experiencing extreme helplessness. Someone may have no choice but to eat meat that was not slaughtered in the Name of God.

Later in Chapter 6 in verse 145 the types of food that are forbidden to the Muslim are listed. Muslims are forbidden to eat carrion, fried blood (blood in general), pig meat or meat slaughtered not in the Name of God. It was common amongst the pagan Arabs to eat fried blood and the consumption of pig is common in most non-Muslim societies. Again, this verse points out that if one is compelled to eat these things there is no crime upon him. These injunctions are repeated in Chapter 16 verse 115.

There is an interesting verse in the Gospels about the eating of food which is commonly used as a Christian refutation of the need to remain kosher or, in Islamic terminology, *halal*. Matthew 15:11 and Mark 7:15 state that it is not what enters the mouth that makes a person dirty, but it is what comes out of the mouth. Despite the assertion that Jesus did not come to change the Law it appears that this is a refutation of that Law. Was Jesus simply making a point?

In Matthew 15:18-20 Jesus clarified his point that those things that come out of a person's mouth come from his/her heart which causes the person to defile him/herself. In particular, Jesus was not talking about pork which is commonly misunderstood to be given permission in this passage. In verse 20 he indicated that he was specifically talking about eating without washing the hands. In Jewish society it was obligatory to do so before eating. In Islamic society it is stressed, but not obligatory.

Avoid Shameful Deeds (Sexual Crimes)

Sexual crimes are considered shameful deeds in Islam. In Chapter 6 verse 151 it is commanded that the believer should not commit lewd acts whether it is open or secret. A similar command is repeated in Chapter 17 verse 32 in which adultery is clearly stated as being a lewd act that is evil.

Adultery is a serious crime in Islam. Later in Medina it was an act that became punishable by death. This ruling was never codified in the Qur'an, but the *hadith*. It was a practice that was codified in the Torah in Deuteronomy 22:22 and Leviticus 20:10. In Mecca the point that it was a great sin was being made. In Chapter 25 verse 68 the serious sins are listed such as polytheism and killing one's children out of fear of poverty (abortion or infanticide). Among these heinous sins fornication is listed which Ibn Kathir explained as committing adultery with the neighbor's wife.

Although the Meccan verses make it clear that adultery is a major crime they also make clear what sexual contact is allowed in Islam. In Chapter 23 verses 5 to 6 are part of the preceding assertion of behaviors that are becoming of believers in verse 1. They abstain from sex except with their wives or their captives. Sexual relations with one's slaves were quite common throughout history. The founding fathers of the United States did it and the Prophet Abraham also did it with his slave-girl Hagar. These two categories were the only permissible avenues for sexual conduct whereas all others were considered crimes.

Sex between unmarried people did not garner the death penalty in Islam, only adulterous relationships between married people.

The teachings of Jesus as contained in the Gospels have a more extreme approach to adultery in which even looking at a woman who is not your wife is considered an act of adultery. In Islam looking at a woman who is not your wife is a sin, but not a major sin like adultery. Jesus explained further in Matthew 5:29-30 that it would be better to remove one's eyes and hands than commit sexual crimes which include staring at women lustfully. This is a powerful exhortation both to Muslims and Christians on the seriousness of sexual crimes.

Greeting of Peace

In Chapter 6 verse 54 the Muslims are told to greet other believers with the greeting '*Salamun Alaikum*' which means 'Peace be Upon you.' Ibn Kathir explained that by offering this greeting one is honoring the person who is greeted with it while also informing them of God's Mercy for them. This greeting is used by Muslims with each other today.

In a section of the story in the Gospel in John 20:19 the disciples were gathered in a building with the door shut because they feared the Pharisees. Jesus came upon them and when he did he offered a greeting, 'Peace be unto You.' This greeting that Jesus used to greet his disciples is the same greeting that Muslims are told to offer each other.

6.1.4. Fairness and Justice

Being fair and being just is a top priority in Islam. Even in Mecca where the Muslims were in no position to enforce any form of justice the Muslims were commanded during this period to be fair and just. Chapter 16 verse 90 states that God commands justice which includes being kind and treating people good, upholding the ties of kinship and being patient rather than punish which Ibn Kathir backed up with references to Chapter 16 verse 126, Chapter 42 verse 40, and Chapter 5 verse 45.

The idea that the Muslims should be more forgiving than seeking retribution is confirmed in one of the Meccan verses cited above by Ibn Kathir. In Chapter 16 verse 126 the permission is given to seek retribution of equal weight in response to harm, but it is stressed that it is better to show patience and leave it to God. A believer receives reward for acting in this fashion in response to harm so long as s/he does so to glorify God alone.

In Chapter 42 verse 40 which was also cited by Ibn Kathir makes the same assertion as the previous verse. The verse immediately following that verse (41) makes it clear that there is no sin if one seeks revenge on the one who wrongs them. It is perfectly just in Islam to seek equal punishment for crimes committed against them. This is not to be mistaken with vigilantism. Later, in Medina the *hudud* (capital punishments) became codified and were only implemented by a judge who found them guilty. Besides, punishments in Islam are subject to the approval of the victim. If the victim or victim's family forgives them thn the state is not permitted to punish them. As already mentioned, forgiveness is better than punishment in the eyes of God.

In Chapter 17 verse 33 and repeated in Chapter 25 verse 68 it is explicitly commanded that no life should be taken except for a just cause. A just cause could be implementing justice as this verse describes or in warfare of which will be discussed later in this book. Unjust killing is any killing outside of these two reasons (justice and war). In Chapter 17 verse 31 one example of an unjust killing is the killing of one's children because of the fear of poverty (abortion or murdering one's children). Children are dependent on their parents and for the parents they are a God-given trust (*amana*) which must be protected. The killing of one's children is considered a great sin. It is such a great sin that it is repeated in Chapter 6 verse 151.

Ibn Kathir in explaining Chapter 6 verse 151 and the part that commands the believers not to take any life except through justice and law noted that the Muslim is not to be killed unless s/he has committed adultery, murder or apostasy. The punishment for adultery and apostasy surfaced in Medina. The punishment for adultery has already been discussed in this book. The rule on apostasy like adultery is based in *hadith* not the Qur'an. It was known in Medina that some people would deliberately convert to Islam to later renounce it in an effort to lead some weaker Muslims astray. That later punishment could be specifically for those people, but became a general ruling for anyone exiting Islam. It would not be appropriate here to debate this ruling which deserves its own book.

As for the non-Muslims, Ibn Kathir explained that they are not to be killed so long as they are peaceful with the Muslims. In Arabic the term *mu'ahid* was given to these non-Muslim populations and it was strictly forbidden to harm them. Those non-Muslim populations that are not at peace with the Muslims but are at war with them, then the rules of war in Islam take precedence. These were dictated in Medina and deserve special attention in another book.

Fairness and justice in the Meccan verses also extends to financial transactions. In Chapter 83 verses 1 to 3 the people who defraud others are addressed. In these verses and those that follow in this chapter they are promised nothing but destruction and loss. The loss that is referred to is the loss in the Hereafter. Ibn Kathir added in his explanation of these verses that the People of Shuayb were destroyed because they cheated others. Shuayb was a Prophet who is discussed in the Qur'an. He and his people are discussed later in this book.

In Chapter 17 verse 35 the believers are told to be fair and balanced in their transactions so they will not be like those who regret as identified in the previous verses. Again this is a form of justice and it was included amongst other verses in Chapter 17 that point to different aspects of justice. In Islam being just and fair is more important than amassing wealth especially if that wealth was acquired through cheating others.

The concept of justice is a part of the Gospels as well. The most famous verse in the Gospels spells out the concept of fairness and justice as conceptualized in Christianity as well as Islam. In Matthew 7:12 it is commanded that the believers do to others as they would have others do to them. This is a great and powerful command that externalizes people's focus on others so that they will understand the effects of their injustice and lack of fairness. Would you like to be cheated, hurt or discriminated against? The assumed answer is 'No.' The resulting advice is not to do it to others if you do not like it.

The commands of Jesus in the Gospels regarding justice involve the judging of others. In Matthew 7:1 and repeated in Luke 6:37 it is commanded that the believers not to judge others as they will be judged. This indicates the imperative in Christianity to forgive the mistakes of others as it is in Islam. It also commands the faithful to avoid passing judgment on the imperfections of others because no one is perfect. It's unfortunate that religious societies lapse into self-righteousness while those who are enthusiastic to prosecute are themselves involved in sins.

Jesus did not mean that there is no judgment on people. People commit crimes and deserve judgment. In John 8:16 Jesus stated that he is the one who can judge because he judges on behalf of the commands of God. This indicates that judges who are sanctioned, i.e. are educated in the heavenly law and observe it, have the right to judge others. Judgment on other people in Christianity and Islam is not to be left to just anyone. The central role of the judge in Christian and Muslim societies is evident even today although the potency of God's Law today in these proceedings is shrinking.

6.1.5. Integrity

A part of being fair is also maintaining one's integrity. In the Meccan verses it is emphasized that the Muslims keep their promises. The Prophet even before his Prophethood was known as *al-Amin* or the Trustworthy. He was a tradesman who was trusted with people's merchandise. He always kept his promises. This quality is emphasized through various verses in the Qur'an.

Fulfill Promises

In Chapter 17 verse 34 amongst the other verses discussed in this chapter is a short phrase. It says in the Yusuf Ali translation, "...and fulfill (every) engagement, for (every) engagement will be enquired into (on the Day of Reckoning)."[58] Ibn Kathir explained that this means that the Muslims are commanded to keep their promises. This

---

[58] Ali, A. Y. (2010). *The Meaning of the Glorious Qur'an*. Istanbul, Turkey: ASIR Media. (p. 188).

section of verse 34 explains that the keeping of promises will be asked about on the Day of Reckoning / Judgment.

The command to not break promises is taken a step further by commanding the believer to not break oaths. In Chapter 16 verses 91 to 92 there are commands to fulfill the covenant with God and fulfill promises and oaths to other people. Another issue is also surfaced in these verses. Some people use their oaths to trick others which the Muslims are commanded not to do. As a matter of fact it states in these verses that adherence to their oaths is a test from God. Keeping one's oaths is a good deed. Not keeping one's oaths is a bad deed.

In the Gospels in Matthew 5:33-37 the swearing of oaths is actually discouraged. In verse 37 it is emphasized that a person should just confirm that they will do it or not do it without swearing to do it.

6.1.6. Repentance

In Islam the door to forgiveness is always open. All of these topics covered in this section involve commands to do or not to do something. If one does something that is forbidden to be done or does not do anything that they should they can change and seek repentance. In Chapter 7 verse 153 it is emphasized that if one has done wrong, then they must seek repentance and believe thereafter. In this verse two of the names of God usually associated with forgiveness are used. God is referred to in this verse as the Oft-Forgiving and the Most Merciful.

Repentance is also an important topic in the Gospels. Luke 15:7 notes that the heavens are in joy over the repentance of one sinner than many righteous people who do not need to repent. In this verse the sinner who changes his life and repents has more weight than 99 righteous people. This importance given to repentance is also communicated in a story in Matthew 21:28-32 in which a father had two sons in which he asked each of them to work in the vineyard. One of them told his father he would not do it while the other son told him that he would do it. The one who resisted the work eventually repented and went to the vineyard to work while the one who said he would do it actually did not do it. Jesus then asked his audience, the Pharisees, which of the two sons did the will of his father and they affirmed that the first son who repented. Jesus then told them that the sinners will go to heaven before the Pharisees will, because they rejected Prophet John while the sinners accepted him and repented for their crimes.

6.1.7. Migrate to a Better Place

In Chapter 29 verse 56 the Muslims are commanded to migrate to a place where they can practice Islam. This verse was revealed to encourage the first migration from Mecca to another place where the Muslims would not be oppressed. This first migration was to Ethiopia where some Muslims, not all, migrated to escape the tortures of the Meccans.

The next time there was a migration it was to Medina in which most of the remaining Muslims along with Muhammad left to go to Medina officially ending the Meccan period and beginning the Golden Age of Islam. This final command to migrate was given in the form of a prayer in Chapter 17 verse 80. This would be the last verse in the Meccan period.

The command to migrate from places where the believers are being oppressed can also be found in the Gospels. Matthew 10:23 states that when they are persecuted in one city they are to flee to another city. This is very similar to the command that came to the Muslims when they were being persecuted in Mecca. The early Muslims did flee to another city as did Jesus and his followers, although unlike Muhammad, Jesus was never able to establish a foothold anywhere throughout Greater Palestine before he departed the world.

6.2. The Commands: The Qur'an

6.2.1. Belief and Behaviors

There are several concepts discussed in the Meccan verses that are not addressed in the Gospels that deserve mention in this chapter. There are a number of recommended beliefs and behaviors that define Islam and its practices. The first and most obvious in this book until this point is the rejection of polytheism which is emphasized throughout the Qur'an, but especially in the Meccan period. There are other commands such as dressing appropriately, avoiding mischief, keeping close with the community of believers while being gentle with them and avoiding envy that are also mentioned in the Meccan verses. Many of these commands can be found in the Old Testament of the Bible, but not in the Gospels. It may have been common knowledge amongst the people of Jesus hence the reason he did not specifically address it. The people of Mecca were still very polytheistic and given to many of the vices that are addressed in this section.

No Polytheism

In Chapter 6 verse 151, the first thing that is listed as a prohibition is joining anything with God as His equal. This verse lists a number of prohibitions in which Ibn Kathir cited Dawud al-Awdi who narrated what al-Sha'bi said which, "Al-qamah said that Ibn Mas'ud said, 'Whoever wishes to read the will and testament of the Messenger of God on which he placed his seal, let him read these verses.'"[59]

This will and testament cites the prohibition of polytheism first in which Ibn Kathir explained that someone who rejects polytheism and worships God alone will receive Heaven. As this verse highlights this point is the most important before any of the other actions. One can be kind to his parents, preserve the life of his children and refrain from murder, but for a whole recognition of his good deeds it is necessary that he worships God alone and no other.

In Chapter 7 verse 33 the emphasis on monotheism is made again although this time it is listed after avoiding shameful deeds, sins and rejecting truth. In Chapter 25 verse 68 it is placed again at the beginning of the listing of crimes to avoid. In this verse the believer is instructed not to call on anyone except God, i.e. do not pray to anyone or anything except God.

---

[59] Ibid.

In Chapter 30 verses 31 to 32 those that follow the straightway are referenced. This straightway includes the worship of God alone. In verse 32 this way is juxtaposed to those who create sects which accept some things and reject other things when they should accept Islam in whole not part. Ibn Kathir explained that the Prophet Muhammad predicted that the future Muslims would do this like other religious communities. Some of these communities have included very polytheistic elements in their understanding of Islam.

In Chapter 72 verse 18 the places of worship are addressed in which they are for the worship of God alone. In Chapter 7 verse 180 the worship of God means referring to Him by His many names. In Islam there are 99 common names of God which describe His attributes. Most of these names can be found in the Qur'an and others in the *hadith*. In this verse when people profane these names the believers are commanded to leave those people. The point is that the accuracy of who to worship is stressed in this rejection of polytheism and that this pure worship is out of respect for the One God.

Dress Appropriately

In Chapter 7 verse 31 the believers are commanded to clothe themselves properly at the places of worship. People in any religion are expected to wear their best clothes to their respective places of worship. This concept is like when we choose the right dress for a certain setting. The goal is to appear as appropriate as would fit to the majesty of God. While it is enjoined to dress well at the places of worship it is further commanded to avoid extravagance because God does not love those who spend recklessly and wastefully.

The purpose of clothing is expanded upon in Chapter 7 verse 26. Ibn Kathir explained that clothes have two parts. The inner parts cover the private parts (inner clothes – underwear) and the outer parts are for the purposes of beautification. These are essential and complimentary respectively. Clothes serve a purpose, i.e. to preserve one's modesty. One can beautify themselves with clothes as much as they like, but they are advised to avoid extravagance.

Creating Mischief

In general, in Islam, mischief is forbidden. In Chapter 7 verse 56 it is commanded that people do no mischief on the Earth but instead fear God and seek His mercy. Islam is about order as are most religions. Religions structure life to create flow and cooperation, not utopia. This aids in developing a cohesive society. Violations of those rules create mischief that can tear that society apart.

Stick with the Believers

One of the methods to avoid being those who create mischief and violate the laws of God is to stick closely with those who value those laws and adhere to them. The old adage that *one is known by the company they keep* takes on religious meaning in Chapter 18 verse 28. This verse was direct advice to the Prophet Muhammad which indirectly serves as advice to all Muslims.

Ibn Kathir explained this verse by pointing out that the nobles of Mecca worked to separate the weaker Muslims (poor, ex-slaves and generally those from a weak tribe) from the Prophet's side. The Prophet worked tirelessly to get the nobles of Mecca to embrace Islam. The leaders of Mecca would scoff at the idea of affiliating with a religion that at that time was composed of the lowest members of Meccan society. The Prophet was commanded in this verse to stick with those that remember God and not be distracted by those who have wealth and power but forget God. This command carries forth to today. The best connected and wealthiest people are not always the best people to be around if one wants to obey God.

Be Gentle with the Believers

In Chapter 15 verse 88 the same idea as the previous section surfaced regarding the need to focus on those that follow God. This verse also was directed at the Prophet, but applies to all Muslims. He was told in this verse that he was not to focus on the world and all of its pomp. Some men/women are quite rich and are living a life of great extravagance and have greater power. It is completely understandable why anyone would want this life. People kill for it in every age.

Instead, this verse refocuses the believer back on the top priority which is other believers and the shared belief in the One God. If the Muslims are poor, uneducated or appear to be rough around the edges this is not a cause for someone to scorn them. In this verse they are commanded to be gentle with them and give them the honor that is due to them.

No Envy

One of the reasons that believers are told to keep their focus on other believers and avoid dwelling on the splendor of others is because of the Islamic emphasis on not being envious of others. In Chapter 20 verse 131 they are again advised not to become centered on the splendor of those that are trapped by this life and its wealth. The believers are reminded that the Hereafter is much better in provision than this life.

Ibn Kathir explained this verse through a *hadith* that describes an occasion when Umar, one of the prominent companions of the Prophet, entered the living quarters of the Prophet and saw him sleeping on a cheap mat. Umar felt sad because great men like the kings of Rome and Persia slept in great palaces with extravagant bedrooms and the Prophet who was greater than these men slept on a mat on the floor. The Prophet told Umar not to be confused on the meaning of wealth which in Islam is only a test. As a matter of fact, the Prophet feared for the Muslims the acquisition of wealth because of what impact this would have on them.

6.2.2. Integrity

In the Meccan verses it is emphasized that the Muslims not only keep their promises, but not to lie as well. The Prophet Muhammad was known for keeping his promises and never lying. His trustworthiness and truthfulness were characteristics of Muhammad that makes the rejection of his message by the Meccan elite surprising. All Prophets were of this character. Again the reason why it is not found in the Gospels that the community of believers was commanded to not lie is probably because the Old Testament, i.e. the Torah already addressed this issue and it was widely known and accepted as a valid command.

No Lies

Chapter 25 verse 72 explains what believers in Islam do not do. As Ibn Kathir explained regarding this verse the believers are not to bear witness to falsehood which includes lies, foul speech and false words. They do not do any of these things nor do they give audience to anyone engaged in this behavior.

The injunction not to bear false witness is repeated in Chapter 17 verse 36. In this verse the Muslims are commanded to not say anything of which they have no knowledge. Just as it was stated in verse 34 it states again in this verse that every act of hearing, seeing and feeling will be asked about in the Hereafter. Testifying to falsehood is one of those things that will be a problem for someone when they face judgment.

6.3. Summary

In both the Qur'an and the Gospels there are a number of commands that resonate with each other. They enjoin their followers to forgive and be patient with those that harm them while it is added in the Meccan verses of the Qur'an that the Muslims are to forgive those who do not believe in Islam for their ill behavior as well as only saying those things that are good in the face of the bad behaviors of those who do wrong. While both the Qur'an and the Gospels enjoin the believers to be kind and forgiving, the Qur'an also adds that it is fully permissible to seek equal retribution for a crime committed against them.

In the Gospels as it is in the Qur'an the believers are told to invite those who do not believe to embrace the message of the one true God. Initially, in the Gospels Jesus made it clear that he was only preaching to the People of Israel while the Qur'an from the beginning was to be preached to anyone following the period of secrecy in the first three years. The Qur'an adds that the believer is to invite to Islam in the best way without insult or injury in which conversion to Islam is purely voluntary. The person who does this is considered the best person amongst the people.

There are a number of emphasized beliefs and behaviors in the Qur'an and Gospels that are similar, and in some cases exactly the same. In the Qur'an the idea of personal responsibility for one's deeds is emphasized which can also be found in the Gospels. The parents are to be respected, whereas the Gospels hint at approval for the Old Testament ruling of death for those children who disrespect their parents. Both the Qur'an and the Gospels stress not being arrogant, avoiding sexual deviations and greeting each other with the statement 'Peace be upon you.' The Qur'an specifically mentions types of food that can be eaten while Jesus's singular reference to eating is not clear enough to say that Jesus invalidated the kosher rules of the Torah. The Qur'an alone again emphasizes the importance of staying away from polytheism while emphasizing that the Muslims should stick together and be kind to each other. Further the Qur'an stresses the importance of avoiding mischief, not envying others and dressing properly at places of worship.

The importance of keeping one's oaths is covered in both the Qur'an and the Gospels while the Gospels go a step further and actually forbid oath-taking possibly for the reason that oaths were frequently broken at the time of Jesus. The Qur'an adds that the Muslims are not to be false or say anything about what they do not know. These two messages also point out that if one is a transgressor such as one who breaks his/her oaths then repentance is necessary to achieve Heaven.

Interestingly, in both the Qur'an and the Gospels there is emphasis placed on migrating from places where the believers are oppressed. Even in the stories of these two men, migration was a frequent occurrence for them. Jesus migrated more than Muhammad did in which Muhammad only migrated once to Medina while Jesus migrated from town to town frequently.

CHAPTER 7

REWARDS FROM GOD

Rewards from God

The rewards bestowed on mankind from God are numerous. Often people are caught looking at all the negative aspects of life, but they fail to see all the blessings they have received. In this chapter there are a number of verses that were revealed in Mecca that explain how God rewards people and gives them many blessings. The ultimate blessing is Heaven, but even while one lives in this life there are many things that bring pleasure. Some of these verses focus on how God rewards those who follow His commands. Other verses console people who are experiencing distress. Throughout these verses it becomes apparent that one of the greatest blessings given to mankind is the Mercy of God of which without it people would be lost.

7.1. The Rewards from God: The Qur'an and the Gospels

7.1.1. God's Blessing

In Chapter 16 verse 18 it is challenged that even if someone wanted to count all the blessings given to them by God they would never be able to do it. This indicates that these blessings are uncountable. This is a profound statement because most people only know the bad things that have happened to them. They rarely appreciate all the good things no matter how small. This verse reminded the Muslims at that time in Mecca and today that no matter how bad life appears to be the blessings of God are still too numerous to count.

In Matthew 5:3-11 there are a number of people who Jesus described as blessed by God. The poor, the mourners, the meek, the hungry, the thirsty, the merciful, the pure in heart, the peacemakers and the persecuted are all described in these verses as people who are blessed by God. The blessing is that they will get what they do not have now in Heaven. In verse 12 the believers are told to be happy because they will receive Heaven which is the best of rewards for faith and steadfastness.

A similar version of this statement can be found in Luke 6:20-23. The poor, the hungry and the persecuted are the specific categories in these verses that are considered blessed by God. The same verse in Matthew is repeated here in verse 23 in which these trials should not be a cause for lamentation, but rejoice as the reward is Heaven.

Another blessing from God is discussed in the Gospels as well. In Matthew 21:22 it is stated that all things that will be asked for in prayer will be given by God. In the previous verse, 21, it adds that this person must have faith and no doubt. This is a great blessing by God in that people always ask God for many things, but unfortunately they lack the faith and have too many doubts for their prayer to be truly effective.

7.1.2. Everything Is Transitory in This Life

In Chapter 42 verse 36 it is explained that all that one receives in this life is just for the convenience of this life. It does not last. The house that one buys will one day pass to another person once the owner dies. All the money earned will also be given to others. At the end all one takes with him/her is his/her record which is what really mattered all along. Ibn Kathir explained that although everything in life is transitory the reward from God lasts forever, i.e. Heaven.

This is a concept that is emphasized in the Gospels. In Luke 14:33 Jesus exclaimed that if a person wanted to be his disciple s/he had to forsake all that s/he owned in this life. The shedding of worldly possessions is indicative that the life that Jesus was offering was a life based on austerity and commitment to God alone. Although this level of austerity was not demanded from Muhammad, he emphasized the giving away of one's wealth in charity which would only be doubled in the Hereafter. Both Jesus and Muhammad were poor and continued to be poor until the end of their missions despite having many opportunities to use their message and power to amass wealth.

7.1.3. Good Deeds / Bad Deeds

In Chapter 23 verse 102 the analogy of the balance is used in regards to deeds. The balance or scale that is heavy with good deeds will determine if one enters Heaven or not. Ibn Kathir explained that even if the scale favors good deeds only by one it will be enough to grant that person Heaven.

The accumulation of good deeds is not made difficult by God. In Chapter 6 verse 160 the multiplication of good deeds over bad deeds supports this idea. A good deed is multiplied by ten while a bad deed only equals one. Even the thinking of doing a good deed is enough to receive that good deed whereas doing it is rewarded by many times. Conversely, the thinking of a bad deed does not earn that person a bad deed.

In addition, the accumulation of good deeds while one is dead is still possible as stated in Chapter 36 verse 12. In this verse it is stated that God records the deeds of everyone and the legacy they left behind in the world. A bad legacy will equal more bad deeds while a good legacy will equal more good deeds. In his explanation of this verse, Ibn Kathir cited a *hadith* that is found in *Sahih* Muslim of the Prophet Muhammad when he said, "Whoever starts (or sets an example of) something good in Islam, will have a reward for it, and a reward equal to that of everyone who does it after him, without that detracting from their reward in the slightest. Whoever starts (or sets an example of) something evil in Islam, will bear the burden for that, and a burden equal to that of everyone who does it after him, without that detracting from their burden in the slightest."[60]

Although the concept of the acquisition of good deeds to achieve Heaven was refuted by Paul and the dichotomy of 'justification by faith' versus the 'justification by works' exists in Christian debates, there is a verse in Matthew 5:16 which stresses the importance of good deeds. In this verse it is stated that the believers are to let their 'light' shine so that men may see the good works that they do and be enticed to worship God. If good deeds were not important in Christian theology then the good works referred to in this verse would not exist. In

---

[60] Quran Tafsir Ibn Kathir - Home. (2010, March). Retrieved from www.qtafsir.com/.

the case of this verse the doing of good works helps people realize the goodness of God. The reason is very worldly while in Islam the reason is mostly projected into the Hereafter so as to obtain Heaven.

7.1.4. Charity Equals Multiple Rewards

The concept of good deeds being multiplied is reflected in the rewards of God being multiplied. The example of the multiple rewards of giving charity is made in the Meccan verses. In Chapter 30 verse 39 the first critique levied at usury on money lending is made. Charity receives multiplied rewards from God whereas the lending of money on interest gains nothing for the lender with God. Later, in Medina the pronouncements against the use of interest were made in stronger terms elevating this practice to forbidden in Islam. Just like the lender receives compounded earnings on lent money, the charity that one gives receives compounded earnings in rewards from God.

In the Gospels in Mark 12:41-44 there is a story about Jesus and his disciples who were watching people submit charity to the treasury. There were a lot of rich contributors, but one poor woman came and donated all that she had with her. Jesus told his disciples in verses 43 to 44 that the poor woman's contribution was greater than the contribution of the rich because she gave all that she had while the rich simply gave from their abundance. The lesson from this story is that it does not matter how much one gives, but the sacrifice of that contribution is the real power of charity. In this life it may appear as a loss, but as pointed out in the Qur'an it will only multiply the rewards toward Heaven for the person who does this.

7.2. The Rewards from God: The Qur'an

7.2.1. Burdens

The blessings of God given to mankind do not mean that people will not experience trials. People get sick, there are wars, people lose their jobs, families are disrupted, natural disasters occur and any number of terrible things could happen. Chapter 21 verse 35 t states that God will test everyone with both difficulty and ease. The purpose of this is to determine who will give thanks and is patient versus those who are ungrateful and are impatient and despair. Ibn Kathir explained that people will be tested both with prosperity and difficulty, health and sickness, lawful and unlawful things, obedience and sin, and guidance and misguidance. For the Muslim this test is the reason for life on this planet.

In Chapter 29 it is also explained that all people will be tested. In verse 2 a rhetorical question is asked whether people think that they will be left alone. This idea is refuted. Ibn Kathir in explaining this verse asserted that these tests are scaled according to their faith, the stronger the faith the stronger the test. Chapter 7 verse 42 clearly states that no soul is ever burdened more than it can bear. This fact is understood to mean that no matter how bad something seems the believer is reassured in this verse that s/he can handle it. Sometimes events feel overwhelming, but the ability of people to overcome these problems has been instilled in each person. The person who despairs or worse commits suicide obviously fails in this challenge.

The concept of God not burdening anyone with more than s/he can bear is repeated in Chapter 23 verse 62. In this verse the concept of the record is explained in that everything that happens to a person will be recorded in a record including how the person reacted. It states that no one will ever be wronged. The suffering of someone in this life could grant them access to Heaven in the next life if they are patient and worship God alone. Ibn Kathir explained that God will forgive and overlook sins in many cases. A bad life is not necessarily a bad thing if the believer can turn the lemons into lemonade and receive Heaven in exchange for this life, after all this life is temporary.

7.2.2. Purify the Soul and Fear God

God guarantees the everlasting reward of Heaven for those who purify their souls and fear God. The fear of God is not the same as fear towards a tyrant. It's more of a fear of misusing the great trust (*amana*) given to each person by God to do right versus wrong. Chapter 67 verse 12 stresses that those who fear God will receive forgiveness and a reward, i.e. Heaven. It also explains in this verse as pointed out by

Ibn Kathir that the best fear of God is that practiced in privacy not trying to show off. Some servants of God spend the night praying and
crying to their God out of their sincere fear of Him. No one ever sees
this. Some do this in public simply to be seen to get recognition for
being pious.

The ultimate objective through this fear of God is to purify the
soul. In Chapter 91 verses 9 to 10 it is stated that those who purify
their souls will be successful while those that corrupt them will fail. Ibn
Kathir explained that by obeying God one purifies his/her soul. He
also reported a *hadith* of Muhammad in which he would stop after
reciting this and say, "Oh God! Give my soul its good. You are its
Guardian and Master, and the best to purify it."[61] Ibn Kathir also
included that Muhammad would make a prayer against weakness, lazi-
ness, senility, cowardliness, stinginess, and the torment of the grave.
These are all negative behaviors and outcomes in Islam.

7.2.3. God Not Quick to Punish

One of the countless mercies and blessings of God on mankind is His
reluctance to punish and His predisposition to give respite for a time.
In Chapter 16 verse 61 it is stated that if God were to punish mankind He would not leave a single living creature on the planet. He
asserts that this will happen one day, but it has a stated term which
cannot be advanced or delayed by even one hour. Ibn Kathir
explained that God is very patient with His creatures and He does
not wish to punish them.

I once wrote an editorial for the *Jakarta Post* while I was living in
Indonesia. Indonesia is a country that experiences frequent natural
disasters. There was a story in the *Jakarta Post* about the leaders in
Indonesia joining together to pray for its safety in which the Director
General for Islamic and Haj Affairs at the Religious Affairs Ministry
noted that the continuous disasters Indonesia was facing at the time
was not a punishment from God, but a test. This is the Islamic theological understanding for natural disasters because as pointed out in

---

[61]　Ibid.

my editorial and in this verse these natural disasters are not punishments, but tests because if God wished to punish a people He would wipe them off the face of the Earth as He has done to generations in the past.[62]

The respite that God grants His creation particularly mankind, who have largely turned their back on Him, is again pointed out in Chapter 10 verse 11. God will not quicken the punishment out of His Mercy although they have earned it. This mercy even extends to prayer as explained by Ibn Kathir. When someone prays for evil, possibly out of anger, God refrains from responding to it. Even in something as intimate as prayer to God, He is still merciful to the one who defiles it. This explanation of Ibn Kathir is repeated for Chapter 17 verse 11 where prayer is explicitly referenced.

7.2.4. Satan Has No Power

One of the greatest blessings and rewards for those who believe in God and follow His commands is immunity from the Devil. In Islam the inclination to do evil has two sources. The first source is the rebellious soul that pushes the person to follow their desires. The second source is the whispers of the Devil and his allies. In Islam the Devil is not an angel as angels are not given a choice to disobey. He is another creation called a *jinn* which was created before mankind. His story according to Islam is explored in the next chapter.

In Chapter 16 verse 99, which is a continuance of verse 98, the believers who trust in God are protected from the motivations of the Devil. In verse 98 it is those who read the Qur'an seeking protection from the Devil that are protected from his influences. The Devil will not have any authority over these people i.e. to make them sin. This is a great reward from God because if one is helped in avoiding sins then the scale of good deeds will get heavier than the bad deeds.

---

[62] Hummel, D. (2007, March 16). Are disasters punishment or test of faith? *Jakarta Post [Jakarta, Indonesia]*. *Retrieved from groups.yahoo.com/neo/groups/suarakorbanbencana/conversations/topics/1327*.

7.3. Summary

In this chapter the rewards of God outlined in the Gospels and the Qur'an are considered together. In the Qur'an the blessings of God are considered to be uncountable while in the Gospels Jesus outlines how those who are considered disadvantaged in this life are still blessed by God especially since Heaven is the greatest blessing anyone could receive. In both the Qur'an and the Gospels this life is considered transitory in that the next life is the only thing of permanence in which Heaven is worth striving for and is the greatest reward of God.

The importance of good deeds is stressed in both the Qur'an and the Gospels although more so in the Qur'an. In the Qur'an it points out that God multiplies these good deeds over the bad deeds in that having more good deeds than bad deeds is necessary to enter Heaven. One of the methods to attain good deeds both in the Gospels and the Qur'an is through charity. In the Gospels it stresses that it is not how much you give, but how much you give as a percentage of your wealth. Islam also has a similar concept to this as well.

The Qur'an alone adds that people are tested in this life in order to determine their faithfulness towards God. These people are tested according to their faithfulness and they are never burdened more than they can bear in this life. One of the results of these burdens when one is faithful and patient is the purification of one's soul through the fear of God which results in the everlasting reward of Heaven.

Despite the preoccupation with the Hereafter in these rewards it is further pointed out in the Qur'an that God is more apt to give respite than to punish people in this life. He is more interested in protecting His creation than causing them harm. In the Qur'an it states that if the believer trusts and believes in God and reads the Qur'an hoping for His protection He will protect them from mankind's greatest enemy, the Devil.

CHAPTER 8

STORIES & PARABLES

Stories & Parables

T he Qur'an, like other religious texts, has many stories and parables that communicate lessons and morals. In the Gospels,
Jesus often spoke in parables which confused those weak in
faith. He did not talk much about former Prophets and/or tell stories
of former people though. In the Meccan verses in the Qur'an there are
many stories and parables.

This chapter is separated into five sections. Sections 1 and 2 are
focused on the Gospel and Qur'anic accounts of Jesus's life and the parables that can be found in both books, respectively. Sections 3 to 5 are
only verses from the Qur'an. The third section is stories that are not
linked to any Prophet. The exception would be the story of the fall of
Adam. Adam is considered a Prophet in Islam. The fourth section is
focused on stories that address a specific Prophet with the exception of
Jesus who is addressed in the first section. These stories are ordered
chronologically based on Islamic accounts. Some of these Prophets are
only referenced in the Qur'an while some can also be found in the Old
Testament of the Bible. The stories are similar with some differences in
the account. The fifth section concerns stories about people who are not
Prophets, but wise men. These men have inspiration, but not revelation.
One of these wise and Godly men interacted with Moses in one story.

8.1. The Story of Jesus in the Qur'an and the Gospels

Jesus is featured in the Meccan verses most prominently in Chapter 19
which is named after his mother. Ibn Kathir explained that this story
is mentioned to show the might, power and ability of God. The conception of Jesus without a father is reinforced in the Qur'an. As Ibn
Kathir explained, Jesus was the culmination of several types of creation

by God. Adam was created with no mother or father, Eve was created from man, but no mother. Mankind in general has both mother and father while Jesus came from a woman with no father.

The story starts in verse 16 where Mary retires away from her family in the East. Ibn Kathir explained that this was the eastern side of the temple in Jerusalem. While there she was approached by what looked like a man, but was actually an angel. She was alarmed, but reassured by the angel that she would bear a son even though no man had touched her.

She then relocated to a remote place where she bore Jesus. After his birth she returned to her people who immediately criticized her thinking she bore the child out of wedlock. Mary had before received a command from God to fast and not speak to any person. Mary could only direct her people to the child, Jesus, who spoke to the people declaring that he was a servant of God and he worshipped Him. He also informed them that he was commanded to make prayer and pay charity. These claims of Jesus as a newborn were nothing short of miraculous, but he repeated it throughout his life. In Chapter 43 verse 63 Jesus confirmed that he was a Prophet and that he had come to explain both religious and worldly matters. In the next verse he confirmed that God is his Lord and that he is His servant. The story in Chapter 19 ends at verse 34.

The story of the birth of Jesus in the Qur'an differs from the account in the Gospels. The accounts in those Gospels that report the event differ from each other. In Matthew the story starts with Mary and Joseph together and Mary had a child conceived already. Joseph wished to divorce her thinking she had conceived the child in an extramarital affair. An angel then approached him in a dream informing him of what was happening. They retired to a house in Bethlehem where the baby was born. After a visit by wise men the family fled to Egypt to escape the wrath of King Herod. Once this king died the family returned to the Galilee to a city called Nazareth. This is the end of the childhood story of Jesus in Matthew.

In the Book of Luke Jesus' family was already in Galilee in Nazareth. In this account the angel approached Mary to inform her of the birth of a son which Mary struggled to comprehend. The angel explained that all is possible with God which she accepted as truth.

A census was then carried out by the Roman Caesar. Jesus' family returned to Bethlehem to be registered for the census. While there Mary gave birth to Jesus. The family had to reside in a manger because the local inn was too full. In this account they were visited by shepherds while there.

Joseph and Mary than brought him to the temple which created a stir amongst the priests and priestesses there. After this they returned to Nazareth where Jesus grew up. There is one additional story in Luke of Jesus as a boy in the temple asking questions of the learned men there, but after this it skips to his ministry which Luke claims started at the age of 30.

The beginning of the story of Luke accords with the Qur'anic version, but the rest cannot be found anywhere in the Qur'an. Matthew and Luke also differ from each other on the account. The story of Mary having the child in the Qur'an did not involve Joseph, kings, wise men/shepherds or forced migrations. In addition, Jesus spoke as an infant which is something that cannot be found anywhere in the Biblical accounts.

8.2. The Parables in the Qur'an and the Gospels

The stories of events in the past, of the Prophets and of the wise men all serve a purpose for instructing the reader in ways to live one's life. Jesus spoke mostly in parables as it states in Matthew 13:34. He spoke with so many parables that his disciples asked him about it in Matthew 13:10. Jesus answered in verse 11 and Mark 4:11-12 that the purpose of speaking in parables was to separate the believers from the non-believers. The non-believers do not understand them because the 'mysteries of the kingdom of heaven' were not given to them. As Jesus cryptically explained in Matthew 25:29, those who were given (knowledge and faith) will receive even more (i.e. Heaven) and those who were not given these things will lose even what they have (i.e. what they earned in this life (material possessions) when they die). This is reinforced in a parable on the king giving coins to his servants in his leave in Luke 19:11-27 in which this concept is explicitly repeated in verse 26.

There is a different explanation for the purpose of parables in the Qur'an. In Chapter 39 verse 27 it is explained what the purpose of parables are to mankind. They are to explain things to mankind by bringing the meaning of the inspiration closer to the minds of people. They are to receive admonition through these parables and call them to memory when needed in life's situations.

Further, the purpose of parables is expressed in Chapter 7 verse 58 which is more of a metaphor meant to explain the effects of revelation from God. This is a parable on guidance and knowledge in which 'clean and good soil' produces good produce while 'bad soil' produces bad produce. This is a verse that refers directly to the effects revelation from God has on people. For those who are good it produces a good civilization, but for those who are bad it produces a bad civilization. This is closer to the rationale for parables as explained by Jesus.

The concept of good soil producing good fruits is explained through a parable in Jesus' explanation of his reasons for speaking in parables. In Matthew 13:3-8 Jesus told the story of a sower who was distributing some seed. Some of the seeds fell to the side and were eaten by birds, some fell on stony places where they could not grow, some fell in sunny areas and were scorched by the sun, some fell in thorny areas in which the weeds choked them out and some fell on good ground and brought up good fruit. Jesus explained this parable in Matthew 13:18-23 in which the seeds that fall to the side are those who hear the word of God, but do not understand it and are caught by the wicked. The seeds that fall in stony and sunny places are in a similar circumstance as they do not benefit from the words of God, but attempt to benefit from it except when persecution reaches them and they abandon the words of God, i.e. they give up and die. The seeds that fall in thorny places are those people who hear the word and understand it, but the allure of riches prevent them from embracing it and acting upon it. Lastly, the seeds that land on good ground are those people that hear the word and understand it while they embrace it and act upon it. Jesus, through this parable, explained the varieties of responses that can be had from hearing a parable.

The concept of ill-growth through ill-actions and beliefs is addressed again in the Qur'an. In Chapter 68 verses 17 to 33 the parable of the People of the Garden can be found. The People of the Garden were not grateful to God for what He gave them, i.e. their garden plus they sought to withhold their produce from the poor. When they returned the next morning to collect their produce they found it destroyed, i.e. turned to dust. At the end of this parable they begin to turn towards God with obedience and remorse for their past beliefs and actions. The lesson to be learned from this parable is that God punishes those who oppose the commands of God, are stingy with the favors of God by withholding the rights of the poor upon them and by being ungrateful to God for all His Blessings.

In a parable on gardens and produce Jesus made a similar point through another parable. In Luke 12:16-21 a rich man took pride as the People of the Garden did with his produce on his farm. He produced so much in fact that he had to consider building a bigger barn. He was so proud of his produce that he thought that from here on out all he had to do was sit back and enjoy. The reality was that on that night he died and the real produce, the treasure with God, was actually empty with this person.

Jesus told two additional parables that illuminate the importance of good deeds and faith. In Luke 10:29-37 Jesus told the story of the good Samaritan. A man was attacked on the road and passed by seemingly righteous people such as a priest. A Samaritan, a person in Israelite society considered to be immoral and reprehensible, stopped and helped him. Jesus made the point in this parable that identity is not important, but deeds / actions are important. Faith without action only reveals weak faith whereas actions with weak faith are also not beneficial to the person or society either.

Actions with weak faith are criticized with the parable of the 10 virgins in Matthew 25:1-13. There were 10 virgins, 5 that were wise and 5 that were not. The 5 wise virgins actively prepared by making sure their lanterns were well-fueled while the not-so-wise virgins did not.

When midnight came the not-so-wise virgins had to set out to find fuel for their lanterns while the wise virgins already had the fuel they needed. While the not-so-wise virgins were searching for fuel the wise virgins met their bridegroom and were ushered inside. When the not-so-wise virgins returned with fuel it was too late to enter. The house represents heaven, the bridegroom, for Christians, is Jesus who shows them the way in, the fuel is the good faith / deeds needed to gain access to heaven and the midnight is the Day of Reckoning / Judgment.

Jesus used another analogy about weak faith in the Gospels in Matthew 7:24-27. In these verses Jesus described the person who follows the sayings of Jesus versus the person who does not follow them. The person who follows them is like a person who builds his house on a rock which can withstand all of the elements, i.e. the assaults on faith. The person who does not follow them is like a person who builds his house on sand which falls under the pressure of the elements.

A similar analogy is made in the Qur'an. Instead of a house on sand, the spider's web is used to symbolize a weak structure, i.e. weak faith. In Chapter 29 verse 41 those who worship other gods besides God hold onto a weak bond like that of a spider's web which is considered the weakest of structures. Later on in Medina a group of hypocritical Muslims supported by one of the foremost enemies to the Prophet Muhammad, Abu Amir, built a mosque which was intended as a base of support for Muhammad's enemies as well as a cause for division in the Muslim community. Muhammad received a revelation regarding this mosque en route to Tabuk to face an oncoming army of Romans. This mosque was described in Chapter 9 verse 109 as being on the edge of a bank about to collapse into the fires of Hell. The mosque in Medina established by Muhammad was established on faith in God and was secure, but this mosque was established on enmity, hatred and disbelief and was therefore insecure. The companions of the Prophet eventually destroyed this mosque.

Parables might represent tests of faith in both Christianity and Islam. The importance of understanding them and acting upon them has major ramifications for such important things as gaining access to Heaven. This is pointed out in John 16:25 in which Jesus exclaimed that one day he will not speak in proverbs. It is indicated that this day is the Day of Reckoning / Judgment in which the veil between this life and the next will be lifted. As pointed out through the various parables discussed in this section belief and action at this time will be pointless so the need for parables will disappear. People will be judged by God as understood in both Christianity and Islam and they will receive their proper rewards/punishments.

8.3. The Stories in the Qur'an

8.3.1. Stories

The stories found in the Qur'an circulate around people and events that focus on those who disobeyed God. The result of this disobedience is the conclusion of these stories which is meant to teach people who believe in God and fear Him the ramifications of their actions. The first of these stories is the fall of the Devil and Adam. In Islam, Adam's ill choice is what locks mankind on Earth until its demise. Adam's mistake in following the Devil was the first mistake of mankind that reverberates until this day.

There are a number of other stories that address groups of people such as the tribes of Israel and the people of Dhu Nuwas who disobeyed God and received His punishment. The story of Dhu Nuwas is largely derived from Qur'anic exegesis than the actual words of the Qur'an. There are also individuals who were not Prophets that did wrong and were either denounced or punished in these stories. These stories focus on the appeals of this life and how it can lead believing men/women astray. In the case of the stories in the Meccan period the appeals of life can either be money or power/prestige. Given the circumstances surrounding the early Muslims in Mecca the lessons these stories teach are applicable to modern Muslims who live in similar circumstances.

The Fall of the Devil and Adam

The fall of the Devil is linked to the creation of Adam in the Qur'an. In Chapter 7 verses 11 to 18 and Chapter 38 verses 72 to 85 the fall of the Devil is chronicled. Adam was created by God and the angels were instructed by God out of their honor for His glory and magnificence to prostrate before him. The Devil is not an angel in Islam. He is a *jinn*, which is another creation by God that has the power to choose between right and wrong. He was granted a great honor by being elevated to the audience of God amongst the angels. When the angels were told to prostrate before Adam, the Devil refused because he felt that he was better than Adam. This angered God who then cast him out for his disobedience and arrogance. The Devil then pleaded for respite which was granted to him. The Devil's response was that he would dedicate himself to leading the descendants of Adam (mankind) astray. He stated that he will attack people from before them, behind them, to their right and their left.

According to Ibn Kathir's explanation of Chapter 7 verse 17, when he attacks before them he creates doubts about the Hereafter. When he attacks from behind them he entices them in this life over the next life. When he attacks on their right he causes confusion about religion and when he attacks on the left he lures them to commit sins. Ibn Kathir explained further that the one direction he cannot attack from is above because this is secured by God's Mercy.

In Chapter 34 verses 20 to 21 it is stated that Satan proved that he would mislead most people except a few. The history of mankind is riddled with his success, but encouragingly with some of his failures also. As it is stated in these verses, Satan is a test for people in which his intrigues are meant to separate those who truly believe from those that do not. As stated previously, one of the blessings of God to mankind is that the Satan has no real power over anyone, but unfortunately many people willingly submit to his advice.

The first of mankind to be misled by the Devil was Adam. This story immediately follows the fall of the Devil in Chapter 7 verses 19 to 25. Adam and his wife, Eve, were dwelling in the Garden until the Devil enticed them to violate the command of God regarding the tree. They were told not to approach the tree, but Satan informed them that if they approached the tree they would become like angels or live forever. They were deceived by Satan who caused them to approach and taste of the tree. This act caused Adam and his wife to fall from grace.

In verse 23 Adam admitted their error and prayed for forgiveness. Ibn Kathir pointed out that in contrast to the Devil who asked for respite, Adam asked for forgiveness. The Devil was given his respite, but he most certainly will be in Hell someday while Adam was given his forgiveness and some of his descendants will be in Heaven because they also sought God's Forgiveness.

The Tribes of Israel

In Chapter 7 verses 163 to 170 the story of those amongst the tribes of Israel who violated the Sabbath is told. The fish appeared to be more abundant on the Sabbath day than on other days. At this time, the believers were told that they were not to work on this day which included fishing. Some of the transgressors amongst them devised a solution. They would leave their nets in the water on the Sabbath and collect them the following day when they could work. The result was that God transformed these people into apes.

In verses 167 to 170 in the same chapter the tribes of Israel are addressed in general. It discusses how God would continue to afflict them with penalties until the Day of Judgment. He tries them through adversity and prosperity so they will one day turn to Him. The result, as it is discussed in verse 169, is that they are succeeded by evil generations that ignore their book. Verse 170 states that those who hold to the book and establish regular prayer will receive their reward from God.

Bal'am bin Ba'ura

In Chapter 7 verses 175 to 176 there is a story of a man who was a follower of the Prophet Moses. This follower was named Bal'am b. Ba'ura in the Qur'anic exegesis. Moses dispatched him to the King of the Madyan people who occupied the area of the Sinai today. He was instructed to spread God's religion amongst these people, but when he got there the King enticed him away from his religion and he adopted the pagan religion of the King.

In verse 176 this person is compared to a dog which only makes one face no matter what is done to Him. Bal'am should have resisted the vanities presented to him by the King in exchange for his convictions. Unfortunately for him, he will only be remembered as one who rejected God's religion and be one of those in Hell.

Qarun

Qarun was another person who interacted with the Prophet Moses. According to many exegetical works, he was the son of the paternal uncle of Moses. He was also very rich. The people following Moses used to warn Qarun to not exult in his riches, but use his riches to obtain the Hereafter such as giving charity. He rejected this advice because he felt God gave him this wealth because he is a great man with great knowledge.

Some people were impressed with his wealth. Eventually, Qarun was swallowed by the earth in an apparent sinkhole which killed him. After his demise those who admired him recanted out of the fear of God. This story can be found in Chapter 28 verses 76 to 82.

People of the Ditch

The story of the people of the ditch appears in Chapter 85 verses 4 to 8. According to the Qur'anic exegesis, the King of Yemen, Dhu Nuwas, persecuted people in his kingdom who converted to Christianity. The King subscribed to Judaism and his kingdom was founded on that religion. Those who converted to Christianity were thrown in a great pit and were burned as it is stated in verse 8 because they believed in God. Dhu Nuwas was eventually unseated from his throne by the King of Ethiopia who responded to this persecution of Christians. This gave way to the era of Christianity in Yemen.

The Companions of the City

In Chapter 36 verses 13 to 29 the story of the companions of the city is told in which there is some disagreement in Qur'anic exegesis on which city is actually being referenced in these verses. Ibn Kathir argued that the city in question is Antioch in present-day Syria, but noted that there is some disagreement on this conclusion. Either way, the story is clear that the city was sent several messengers in which the king and the people disbelieved in all of them and in addition threatened to kill them.

A man came from another part of the city to help these messengers and prevent his people from killing them. According to Ibn Kathir this man's name was Habib al-Najar and he was very sick, but very charitable with good characteristics. He urged his people to follow the messengers, but his people only responded with brute force killing him. God then destroyed these people and their king for disbelieving in the messengers and killing this man.

8.3.2. The Prophet's Stories in the Qur'an

There are a number of Prophets that are mentioned in the Meccan chapters of the Qur'an. Some of the Prophets mentioned can also be found in the Bible such as Moses, Solomon, Noah, Jesus, Abraham, Joseph and Lot. Some of the Prophets can only be found in the Qur'an such as Shuayb, Hud, and Salih. There are also stories surrounding the life of the Prophet Muhammad.

The stories that surround these Prophets follow consistent trends in receiving revelation, communicating that revelation to a largely disbelieving people and encountering resistance sometimes that is violent. These stories mirror the experiences of the early Muslim community in Mecca. They console those believers as well as the Prophet since these experiences have been had before in other communities. The lesson is that the believers should persevere in the face of persecution like those before them. These Prophets are discussed in chronological order based on their appearance in history according to Islamic sources.

Noah

The story of Noah can be found in two places in the Meccan verses. The most comprehensive telling of the story is in Chapter 11 verses 25 to 48. The other telling of the story is more of a summary in Chapter 26 verses 105 to 121. The rendering of the story in Chapter 11 is summarized here.

The story opens with Noah declaring to his people that he has come with a warning. The leaders of his people rejected him because he was only a person and his followers were considered to be of a low status in verse 27. Noah responded that God had sent His Mercy upon him and he would not chase away those who believe in God. He also made it clear that he was not an angel. He repeated these proclamations several times.

Noah's people responded that they were tired of his arguments and threats and challenged him to bring on the punishment if he was actually speaking the truth in verse 32. Eventually God informed Noah that those who believed were all that would believe amongst his community in verse 36. In verse 37 Noah was instructed to begin work on the Ark. While he was building it the leaders of his people would insult him.

In verse 40 the flood began and the instruction to collect creatures in two, males and females, plus Noah's family and the believers was made. When the water of the flood began to overcome the people Noah's son ran to a mountain which was eventually covered in water and he drowned. Noah's son, whose name was Yam in Qur'anic exegesis, was a disbeliever. During his death Noah asked God about his status because he thought his family would be protected. God responded in verse 46 that he was not of his family and admonished Noah not to be among the ignorant. Noah prayed for forgiveness.

In Chapter 71 verses 26 to 27, the culmination of a lengthy prayer by Noah ends with a prayer that God leave not a single disbeliever on the earth. Noah explained in verse 27 that they would continue to mislead the believers if left alive and would only give birth to unbelievers. Ibn Kathir explained that God answered this prayer by destroying all the unbelievers including Noah's son. Further, Ibn Kathir explained this prayer that Noah was so well-informed by God about his people that he knew that if left alive they would continue to spread disbelief.

Hud

Hud is one of the Prophets mentioned in the Qur'an, but not the Bible. The other Prophets mentioned only in the Qur'an are Shuayb and Salih who are mentioned below. In Chapter 7 verses 65 to 72 and

Chapter 11 verses 50 to 58 the story of Hud appears in the Qur'an. Hud was a Prophet sent to the 'Ad people, who were descendants of Noah who lived in present-day Yemen close to the Oman border. Hud was one of the noblemen / chiefs of his people and he was given Prophethood by God to preach to his people and call them to the One God. The 'Ad people had become polytheists since the days of Noah, who established monotheism in the wake of the Great Flood.

Hud implored them to worship the One God, seek His forgiveness, reminding them of the favors of God before who saved them from the Great Flood and explaining that his preaching this message was for the reward of God alone. His people did not respond favorably. They called him a fool, thought he was insane, demanded he bring evidence and finally challenged him to bring on the punishment from God.

Eventually, Hud declared his innocence of their polytheism having tried to correct their false worship. He absolved himself of his people in which he exclaimed that he did his best to warn them and therefore discharged his duty. God then destroyed the 'Ad people completely by sending a great wind that destroyed everything in its wake except Hud and those who believed with him.

Salih and the Thamud People

In the Meccan verses Salih is introduced in Chapter 91 verses 11 to 14. The story in the Qur'an reports that a Prophet named Salih was sent to a people called Thamud. As usual these people rejected this Prophet. As a final test a she-camel was set amongst their pastures with the explicit instruction that they were not to harm it. Of course they rebelled against this command and through their agent of evil, according to exegetical work the name of their leader and the agent of evil is identified as Qudar b. Salif, they killed the she-camel. This final disobedience caused their destruction as it says in verse 14, "so their Lord, on account of their crime, obliterated their traces and made them equal (in destruction, high and low)"[63]!

---

[63] Ali, A. Y. (2010). *The Meaning of the Glorious Qur'an*. Istanbul, Turkey: ASIR Media. (p. 416).

Abraham

In the Meccan verses there are more references to Abraham than any other Prophet. His story can be found in Chapters 26, 21, 6, 14, 19, 29 and 37. In this section the various pieces of this story is discussed in chronological order starting with Abraham's epiphany that there is only One God and ending with his attempted sacrifice of his first son, Ishmael, who in Islam was also another Prophet that is not discussed beyond the story of Abraham.

In Chapter 6 verse 75 it states that God showed Abraham 'the power and the laws of the heavens and the earth' to reinforce Abraham's gravitation towards monotheism. Abraham then contemplated the heavens and the earth and was shown proofs of God's Oneness. Each natural phenomenon that Abraham contemplated whether it was the stars, the moon or the sun verified that there was no permanent figure except God and it was Him that was the only one worthy of worship.

There is a prayer of Abraham in Chapter 26 verses 69 to 102. Some of the story of Abraham can be inferred from this prayer. The first part is more of a dialogue that Abraham had with his people over what they worshipped besides God. He asked if their idols can hear them or help/hurt them. Abraham's people responded that they worship them because their ancestors worshipped them. Abraham then asserted that God is the Only One who created him and guided him as well as the Only One who fed him and gave him drink. Further, Abraham stated that God is the Only One who healed him when he was sick and He is the Only One that can take life and forgive the faults of mankind.

Abraham's prayer really begins in verse 83 and it continues to verse 87 with some more that appear as statements of reinforcement from verses 88 to 102. Abraham prayed for knowledge and favorable remembrance after his death. He also asked for forgiveness for his father who was a disbeliever. Ibn Kathir explained Chapter 26 verse 86 in his *tafsir* that God granted all these requests except the prayer of forgiveness for his father. Ibn Kathir cited a *hadith* in this same explanation of verse 86 which states that on the Day of Resurrection Abraham's father will be covered in dust and darkness which will confuse

Abraham since he prayed for him. God will respond to him that paradise is only for the believers. This situation is not unlike what Noah experienced with his son.

When Abraham confronted his people about the worship of idols instead of the One God in Chapter 21 verse 52, they responded that it was what their fathers worshipped before them as discussed in Chapter 26 above. Abraham asserted that they and their fathers were in error on this point. Further, in Chapter 29 verses 20 to 22 Abraham tried to explain to his people how God creates life after death in which he created all things including them from nothing. He also explained in these verses that God is the ultimate judge and none can escape Him.

Abraham tried to convince his father, who was also a disbeliever as discussed above, that the worship of idols was foolish because they cannot see or hear anything in Chapter 19 verse 42. Abraham used this argument with his people in general in which he even destroyed the idols while the people were away at a festival leaving the largest idol intact. When the people returned to find their idols destroyed they confronted Abraham about it. Abraham responded in Chapter 21 verse 63 alluding to the biggest idol and asked them to inquire of the affair from it. The people after becoming aware of their confusion on the matter responded with brute force. It was this brute force that Abraham's father warned him about when Abraham confronted him about his worship of the idols in Chapter 19 verse 42. The people then tried to burn him in a great fire which did not work since God, who has control over all things, changed the property of the fire to be cool instead of hot.

After this event, Abraham along with his nephew Lot, who believed in the One God also and was a Prophet, migrated to the area of al-Sham. This area is centered in present-day Syria. It was during this migration that Abraham prayed for a righteous son in Chapter 37 verse 100 in which he was granted Ishmael born of his slave-girl Hagar. He settled them in Mecca in which he prayed in Chapter 14 verse 35 for the city that it would be a place of peace and security. He also prayed that Ishmael and his descendants, referring to the Arabs, would establish regular prayer, be loved amongst some in the nations, be fed in this barren land and in general follow his ways. This prayer was accepted by God.

Abraham would visit Hagar and Ishmael in Mecca from time to time. One of these times Abraham had a vision in which he was slaughtering Ishmael in Chapter 37 verse 102. He told Ishmael about this vision who told Abraham that if it was God's command then he was willing to go along with it. Ishmael was about to be sacrificed when God stopped him. According to Ibn Kathir, Abraham actually was trying to sacrifice Ishmael but the knife would not cut him. Instead, God presented Abraham with a ram to be sacrificed instead.

After this event, God gave Abraham good news of another son, Isaac, in Chapter 37 verse 112, who is recognized as another Prophet of God in Islam. In Chapter 21 verse 72 it is stated that Isaac was bestowed upon Abraham and from Isaac came Jacob, another Prophet mentioned in the story of Joseph in the Qur'an. At the same time Lot, who had emigrated with Abraham to al-Sham, was having problems of his own.

Lot

The story of Lot is another example of a Prophet who was rejected by his people. In Chapter 27 verses 54 to 58 there is a short rendition of the story of Lot. The story starts with Lot admonishing his people who were engaged in deviant sexual practices. In verse 55, Lot asked, "Would ye really approach men in your lusts rather than women?"[64] Lot's people did not appreciate this challenge so they became committed to the idea of expelling Lot and his followers.

God then informed Lot to leave in which Lot and his family left except his wife who remained behind. When they had left God destroyed the people of Lot completely. It is reported in verse 58 that God, "rained down on them a shower (of brimstone)."[65]

---

[64] Ibid. (p. 257).
[65] Ibid. (p. 257).

Joseph

The story of Joseph is the entire Chapter 12. It starts in verse 4 when Joseph told his father, Jacob, about a dream he had foretelling his preeminence over his brothers and family in which his father warned him not to share this vision for fear of retaliation from his brothers. His brothers, even without this knowledge, still disliked Joseph because of his father's love for him and his younger brother, Benjamin. They decided to banish Joseph and on an outing they threw him down a well where he was found by a caravan and sold into slavery. The brothers told his father that he had been killed by a wolf and had slaughtered a sheep and smeared a shirt with its blood as evidence of the attack. Their father did not believe them and he mourned the loss of Joseph.

Joseph was sold as a slave in Egypt to a man with the title 'Aziz,' who according to Ibn Kathir was a minister in Egypt. This man had good characteristics in which he advised his wife that his stay with them should be made as comfortable as possible in verse 21. In his explanation of this verse, Ibn Kathir noted a tradition from Abu Ishaq, from Abu Ubaydah, from Abdullah b. Masud that 'Aziz' was one of three people in Islamic tradition that had the most insight. The other two was the woman of the Madyan people who requested her father to hire Moses after fleeing Egypt after the murder of the Egyptian soldier and Abu Bakr when he appointed Umar as his successor to the *Caliphate*.

When Joseph matured he was of sound mind and perfect body. His beauty attracted the attention of Aziz's wife who tried to seduce him one day in the house. Joseph tried to escape her, but she grabbed the back of his shirt on the way to the door and ripped it. Aziz was standing at the door and the two accused each other of wrong-doing while Aziz used the evidence of the shirt torn in the back that his wife had been the instigator of this affair.

This event became the talk of the town in which the women of the city began to gossip of the attempt by Aziz's wife to seduce her slave-boy. She became aware of this gossip and decided to have a banquet for these women where she would show Joseph to them to exonerate her lustful feelings for him. When Joseph was shown to the women they were so infatuated with his beauty that they cut their hands with the knives they were using to cut fruit by accident without realizing it. At this point Aziz's wife demanded that Joseph either submit to her or go to jail in which he prayed to God in verse 33 that prison would be better than disobedience to God. In response, Joseph was sent to jail.

In jail Joseph had two cellmates who had visions about their future. They asked Joseph about these vision in which Joseph informed them of their meaning. One of those cellmates would go on to be the King's wine-distiller in which Joseph requested that once he was freed he would speak to the King on his behalf. Unfortunately, this person forgot and Joseph lingered in jail for seven years, according to the explanation of Ibn Kathir.

One day, the King had a vision and he asked his closest advisors to explain to him the meaning of this vision. At this point the wine-distiller remembered Joseph and returned to the jail to ask Joseph the meaning of the vision. When Joseph informed him that it was a prediction of seven years of famine, he returned to the King to tell him the meaning of the vision. The King agreed with the interpretation and requested that Joseph be brought to him. Joseph refused until the matter concerning Aziz's wife was settled in which the King personally investigated the incident. After Aziz's wife admitted her wrong-doing thus exonerating Joseph of any crime, Joseph joined the King's administration as a minister of finance with control over the storage houses.

When the great famine came, Egypt was prepared under the stewardship of Joseph. The famine even affected Canaan where Joseph's family was residing prompting his brothers to come to Egypt to seek aid from the King. Joseph gave the brothers the aid in exchange for some trade that they brought and in secret returned their trade to them. He asked that they return and bring their brother Benjamin with them. They eventually returned with Benjamin, who became informed in private from Joseph that he was their brother. In secret, Joseph placed the King's bowl in Benjamin's bag, and accused them of stealing it. After inquiring about the punishment for stealing which was to be made a slave of the victim the bowl was discovered in Benjamin's bag.

The brothers were then forced to return to their father to inform them of the loss of Benjamin in Egypt. The father then commanded them to return to Egypt to ascertain the fate of Benjamin. When they returned Joseph revealed who he was to them and at that point the brothers admitted their wrong-doing and the preeminence of Joseph over themselves. Joseph then requested that his entire family including his mother and father be relocated to Egypt. Once in Egypt they prostrated before him as it is stated in verse 100, thus confirming his vision at the beginning of the story.

Shuaib and the Madyan People

In Chapter 7 verses 85 to 93 there is the story of Shuayb and his people the Madyan. The Madyan, besides not worshipping God alone, were corrupt in business transactions. They withheld from those who bought and demanded more from those who sold. Shuayb was a Prophet who came to these people asking them to worship God alone and be fair and just in their business transactions.

As the general trend foretells, the leaders of the Madyan much like the leaders of the Thamud rejected the message of Shuayb and much like the people of Lot they were set on expelling Shuayb and his followers unless they converted back to their religion. The end result was that they were destroyed by a great earthquake. As it says in verse 91, "But the earthquake took them unawares, and they lay prostrate in their homes before the morning!"[66]

Moses

The story of Moses is told in Chapter 20 verses 9 to 99. The story starts with Moses living amongst the Madyan people. At this point he was an outcast after having committed the crime of murdering a soldier who was abusing an Israelite. He saw a fire and investigated it in what is called the Valley of Tuwa in the Qur'an. When he arrived

---

[66] Ibid. (p. 106).

at the source of the fire he was addressed by God who then instructed him to go to the Pharaoh to warn him and request that the People of Israel be allowed to go free. This is where another section of
Meccan verses in Chapter 26 verses 10 to 67 starts with the story of
Moses.

At this point in the story there is a dialogue between Moses and
God. After instructing him in the miracles of God granted him such as
turning his walking stick into a snake and showing his hand as glow-
ing white, God told him that Moses was to go to the Pharaoh and
instruct him of his error and demand the release of the tribes of Israel.
Moses became alarmed with this task and began asking for favors from
God such as increasing his courage, making the task easier, improving
his speech and letting him bring his brother Aaron. These requests
were granted to him.

In Chapter 26 verse 14 Moses also feared that if he returned to
Egypt he would be charged for the crime of murder which he committed against one of the Pharaoh's soldiers. These fears were dismissed
by God and he and Aaron were commanded to go to the Pharaoh.
Further in Chapter 20 verses 37 to 41 God reminded him of the blessings he had received from Him before by recounting his story of being
cast into the river and rescued by the Pharaoh's wife. He was then
raised in the Pharaoh's court and remained there until he committed
murder and became an outcast. The Pharaoh reminded him of this also
in Chapter 26 verses 18 to 19 after Moses and Aaron confronted him
with their mission.

Before Aaron and Moses confronted the Pharaoh, God gave
them advice in Chapter 20 verse 44. He told them to speak to the
Pharaoh mildly and softly so that he may incline towards them. As
Ibn Kathir explained they were instructed to talk to him like a close
friend, because close friends listen to each other better than
entrenched enemies.

The Pharaoh did not incline to them though. Instead he became
more insolent. In Chapter 26 verse 29 Pharaoh threatened them with
death for putting any god ahead of him. Ibn Kathir explained that this
is the response of tyrants when rational proof is brought before them.

They only respond with force. Further Moses showed his designated miracles to the Pharaoh which only prompted him to collect his best magicians to challenge Moses.

The magicians were not only outdone, but they embraced the religion of Moses which caused the Pharaoh more grief. At some point Moses and Aaron were given leave with the tribes of Israel. Eventually there was a change of mind and a chase where the story of Moses striking the sea with his rod clearing a path for them is told. Pharaoh pursued them and was drowned. This is where the story ends in Chapter 26. The story continues in Chapter 20.

Moses then went up the mountain to receive further instruction from God, but in his absence the tribes of Israel were led astray by a person called the Samiri in verse 85. He rallied the people to create a golden calf to worship. Moses returned to set them straight and in anger he grabbed Aaron by his beard for letting the people worship this calf. Aaron responded in verse 94 that he feared he would create division amongst the people because they were so united around creating this golden calf. It is also believed that Aaron tried to stop them, but was unsuccessful. Moses confronted the Samiri and then casted him out. Moses then destroyed the calf and asserted amongst the people that the only deity is God. This is the end of the story in Chapter 20.

Solomon

The story of Solomon and his greatness are reported in the Meccan verses in Chapter 27 verses 15 to 44. Much of this story involves the interaction of Solomon with the Queen of Yemen (Saba') who is known in the Islamic literature as Bilqis. The name of this Chapter comes from an event when Solomon and his forces came to a valley where there were some ants. One of the ants began warning the others to be careful of the approaching army. Solomon could hear all of God's creatures. Out of gratitude for this blessing Solomon prayed in Chapter 27 verse 19, "Oh my Lord! So order me that I may be grateful for Thy favors, which thou hast bestowed on me and on my parents, and that I may work the righteousness that will please Thee!

And admit me, by Thy Grace to the ranks of Thy righteous Servants."[67]

Solomon, like his father David who is mentioned in Chapter 34 verses 10 to 11, was given great power in this life. David had a mighty voice in which even the mountains sang his praises of God with him. He also had control over iron. Solomon not only had the power to understand the communication of God's creatures, he also had power over the wind which could take him long distances in a short time which is discussed in Chapter 34 verse 12. David and Solomon were both grateful for all of these powers given to them and strived to be as grateful as possible.

Solomon's gratefulness for God's Blessings extended to the episode involving the Queen of Yemen. Solomon received reports from the birds and one of them, a Hoopoe, informed Solomon of a queen in Yemen who was very powerful, but she and her people worshipped the sun instead of God alone. A story regarding these people is told in Chapter 34 verses 15 to 17 in which they were given great provisions, but they worshipped the sun. Many Messengers had come to them trying to reassert worship in the One God, but these missions ended in failure. Eventually a great flood caused by a breaking dam scattered their people from their once prosperous land.

In response to this news Solomon sent a letter to this queen commanding her to come to him in submission to the true religion. In response, she sent a present of wealth which was promptly rejected by Solomon. Instead Solomon in Chapter 27 verse 37 threatened them with war.

When the embassy from Yemen left Solomon asked his audience who can bring him her throne. One of the *jinns* who Solomon had command over said he could with ease. As explained earlier, *jinns* are creations of God that exist amongst mankind, but are largely unseen. They can choose between right and wrong and are more powerful than people. In Chapter 34 verses 12 to 13 it is stated that Solomon had

---

[67] Ibid. (p. 255).

control over the *jinn*s in which they worked for him building things and other work.

Another person also said that he could bring the throne to Solomon. This person is described in the Qur'an as, "one who had knowledge of the Book." Ibn Kathir in his explanation of Chapter 27 verse 40 noted that this person was a scribe named Asif b. Barkhiya. This is the one who brought the throne of Bilqis to the throne of Solomon. In response, Solomon exclaimed that this is a Blessing of God to test his gratefulness. Solomon at all times strived to be grateful to God for all things that were given to him as stated previously.

Solomon then had the throne disguised so when Bilqis arrived she would not identify it. She was en route to offer up her submission to Islam. When she arrived Solomon pointed out the throne to her, but she and her people had already submitted themselves to Islam. Later, she was invited to enter the palace which had floors so smooth they appeared as water. When she saw this she lifted her skirt to avoid getting it wet. When she discovered it was glass she exclaimed in Chapter 27 verse 44, "Oh my Lord! I have indeed wronged my soul! I do (now) submit (in Islam), with Solomon, to the Lord of the Worlds."[68]

The death of Solomon is described in Chapter 34 verse 14 in which he died unbeknownst to anyone including the *jinn*s who continued to work on his projects. He died while leaning on his staff and a worm which had eaten the staff through caused him to fall revealing that he was dead. As it is stated in this verse, this was meant as a sign to both *jinn*s and men that only God knows the unseen.

Stories of the Prophet Muhammad

There are several stories that surround the life of the Prophet Muhammad in the Meccan verses of the Qur'an. There is a story about an event that caused God's admonishment and stories about two miracles that occurred in Mecca. There are also two stories about the enemies of the Prophet Muhammad.

---

[68] Ibid. (p. 256).

The story about the event that caused God's admonishment involved a blind man. An entire chapter of the Qur'an is dedicated to this event in Chapter 80. As the story goes the Prophet was speaking to a Meccan leader when a blind man who was already a Muslim approached the Prophet seeking some instruction in Islam. According to one interpretation, Muhammad was trying to convince this leader to convert to Islam and became annoyed with the interruption of this blind man whose name was Ibn Umm Maktum. The Prophet frowned and turned away from him. This caused the revelation of this chapter which informed Muhammad not to focus on the rich only, but also the poor. In another interpretation it was the Meccan leader who became annoyed with the interruption of this blind man. Either way, the de-emphasis on status and the emphasis on faith is established in the story.

There were two major miracles that occurred in the Meccan period of Islam that are reported in the Qur'an. The first miracle is the Heavenly Night Journey which is reported in Chapter 17. The event is mentioned only in the first verse of this chapter. The story is that the Prophet was taken to the farthest mosque which is the *Masjid al-Aqsa* in Jerusalem. From there he ascended the heavens and met all the Prophets that have been mentioned in this section with the exception of a few. Further, he received the required prayers during this ascension which became canonized thereafter as the five daily prayers that all observant Muslims do to this day.

The other miracle reported in the Meccan verses had more eye witnesses. This is reported in Chapter 54 verses 1 to 2. The story is that the unbelievers continually demanded a visual sign that Muhammad was a Prophet. Their demands were met when the Prophet had the moon split in half so wide that a mountain separated the two parts. As amazing a miracle this was in the same caliber if not greater as splitting the sea by Moses or the walking on the water by Jesus the unbelievers in Mecca only responded that it was magic.

There were two major enemies of Muhammad: Abu Jahl and Abu Lahab. These two enemies also received attention in the Meccan verses of the Qur'an. An entire chapter was committed to Abu Lahab in Chapter 111. In this chapter Abu Lahab is told to perish and burn in the fires of Hell along with his wife. This strong condemnation is the result of vehement opposition to Muhammad and Islam by Abu Lahab and his wife.

Ibn Kathir reported a story where the Prophet climbed a hill around Mecca and cried out to the people that if he were to tell them that an enemy was coming behind the hill, would they believe him. The people affirmed that they would in which Muhammad then explained that he was sent by God as a warner to them and they should believe this statement as truth as well. Abu Lahab was angry at Muhammad for saying this and shouted up at him that he should perish. This example characterizes the scorn that Abu Lahab directed at the Prophet. His wife also joined in this scorn by laying obstacles in the Prophet's way to cause him injury.

Abu Jahl was also a vehement enemy of the Prophet. In Chapter 96 verses 9 to 19 the 'one who forbids' refers to Abu Jahl according to Ibn Kathir. The incident involved a time when the Prophet was praying at the *Ka'ba*. Abu Jahl approached him and threatened him from praying there. In these verses God admonishes Abu Jahl for this attack on the Prophet.

8.3.3. The Wise Men Stories

There are two wise men featured in the Meccan verses of the Qur'an. These men were not Prophets, but they were endued with knowledge beyond the visual reality. One of these wise men, Khidr, interacted with one of the Prophets, Moses. Luqman is the other wise man whose wisdom is captured in his advice to his son. Although they were not Prophets their wisdom is Prophetic.

Khidr

In Chapter 18 verses 60 to 82 there is a story that starts with Moses searching for Khidr, whose name is known through Qur'anic exegesis. This introduction starts on verse 65. Moses asked if he could follow him to learn of the Higher Truth because Khidr was more knowledgeable than Moses. Khidr initially declined, but after Moses confirmed his commitment to obey him and ask no questions about what he saw Khidr changed his mind.

There were three events that occurred while Moses was under his wing. The first event involved Khidr and Moses receiving a ride on a boat in which Khidr then destroyed it. Moses did not understand so he questioned Khidr about it. Khidr then reminded him about his pledge in which Moses apologized and they continued onwards.

Khidr and Moses then came upon a boy. Khidr killed the boy by decapitating him with his bare hands which understandably shocked Moses who again questioned Khidr about this act. Khidr again reminded Moses about his pledge in which Moses responded that if he broke his pledge again Khidr could leave him.

After this Moses and Khidr came upon a town in which they asked for some food from the townsfolk. The townsfolk refused to feed them so they proceeded until they came upon a wall in the town. The wall was in disrepair so Khidr fixed it. Moses again did not understand in which he again asked Khidr about it. This caused Khidr to announce that he was parting ways with Moses.

Khidr then explained why he did those things before he left. The boat was set to be confiscated by a king and by destroying it he kept the boat within the ownership of the original owners of the boat. The boy was destined for rebellion and ingratitude to God while his parents were faithful people. The wall belonged to two orphans in which there was a treasure buried beneath it so he rebuilt it to protect their treasure.

Luqman

Luqman is another wise man featured in the Qur'an in which he has an entire chapter named after him in Chapter 31. The chapter is not entirely focused on him; his advice to his son is only in verses 12 to 19. The first bit of advice Luqman gave his son was to worship only One God. In verse 14 he advised his son to be good to his parents especially his mother unless his parents try to make him worship other gods.

In verses 16 to 19 Luqman gave more advice to his son. In verse 16 Luqman reminded his son that all actions will be brought forward on the Day of Resurrection no matter how small those actions appear to be in this life. In verse 17 he told him to perform the prayer while forbidding evil and enjoining what is good and just. In this verse he also advised him to endure with patience all things that occur, which according to Ibn Kathir is one of the most important commands of Luqman to his son. In verse 18 it is advised that one is not to be arrogant towards anyone for any reason and the believer should always have a cheerful face. Lastly, in verse 19, Luqman told his son to be moderate in his voice level because loud voices draw parallels with the loud noises of the donkey.

8.4. Summary

The story of Jesus is contained in both the Qur'an and the Gospels. In particular the Gospels of Luke and Matthew contain the beginning story of Jesus which the Qur'an also has within its pages. The only similarities between the Qur'an and the Gospels are at the beginning of the Book of Luke. In addition, the Book of Luke differs from the Book of Matthew.

In the Qur'anic account, Mary went off and was approached by an angel who told her that she would have a baby. In the Book of Luke, this is also how the story begins. From there, the Qur'an tells a story that cannot be found in the Gospels such as when Mary returned and Jesus spoke as an infant on her behalf. The Gospels have more information on the events surrounding the birth of Jesus in which they contradict each other.

The Qur'an and the Gospels both have parables. In the Qur'an, it is explained that parables are meant to bring the meaning of the revelations closer to the minds of people, i.e. increase knowledge of them and bring them to memory. In the Gospels, Jesus explained that parables are meant to separate believers from unbelievers.

In both messages there are parables about the good soil versus the bad soil. In the Qur'an, it is stated that good soil produces good produce while bad soil produces bad produce. The soil can be likened to the souls of men which are either pure or corrupted. The story of the People of the Garden in the Qur'an reinforces this concept. In the Gospels, Jesus used seeds landing in different environments as a parable where those seeds that fall on good soil produce good fruit. The story of the rich farmer in the Gospels also reinforces this concept. The idea is the same between the version in the Qur'an and the Gospels.

In the Gospels there are a number of parables that point out weak faith such as the Good Samaritan story, the story of the ten virgins and those who build their houses on sand. In each of these stories those with weak faith are highlighted to show the results of their weak faith. The Qur'an has a complimentary conception with the spider's web.

The Gospels do not have stories of the former Prophets whereas the Qur'an is full of them. In the Meccan period there are many references to these Prophets. The Qur'an also discusses the fall of the Devil and Adam, the breaking of the Sabbath by the Tribes of Israel and various characters who went astray.

The Meccan verses of the Qur'an also highlight the stories of Moses and his confrontation with the Pharaoh, Solomon and his confrontation with the Queen of Yemen, Noah and his Ark, Abraham and his father, Lot and his sexually deviant people, Salih and the people who killed the She-Camel, Shuayb and his corrupt people, Hud and his polytheistic people and Joseph and his story of preeminence. There are also a number of stories about the Prophet Muhammad in the Qur'an such as the blind man who approached him for religious advice, the miracle of the Heavenly Night Journey, the miracle of the moon-splitting and his enemies Abu Jahl and Abu Lahab.

There are two stories of two wise men featured in the Qur'an. The first is a wise man named Khidr who interacted with Moses who followed him for a time. The other wise man is called Luqman whose advice to his son is reported in the Qur'an.

CHAPTER 9

EXPLANATIONS

Explanations

In the Meccan verses there are many explanations of the way things are in the world and in the religion of Islam. Some of these explanations focus on the Prophets and in particular the Prophet Muhammad and Jesus. Some of the explanations regard the religion sent by God and why there are many religions in the world. There are also explanations on faith that include pre-destination, the trials of life, diversity in life, and the unseen such as the angels and the *jinn*. Lastly, there are explanations on events that have not happened yet, i.e. prophecy.

9.1. The Explanations: The Qur'an and the Gospels

9.1.1. Sending of Prophets

The Qur'an makes it clear that Prophets were sent to all people in Chapter 10 verse 47. The purpose behind sending Messengers to all people is so they will not have an excuse when they face judgment in the Hereafter. When those Prophets were sent according to Chapter 7 verses 94 to 95, those people were tried through adversity and suffering in order that they may learn humility. As noted in multiple places in this book afflictions in Islam are not necessarily punishments from God. They are meant to build the faith of those who experience those afflictions.

In verse 95 it is noted that after this suffering there is prosperity so that the people can be grateful. It is warned in this verse that adversity and prosperity follow a cycle. There is an overhanging purpose to the adversity and prosperity that is meant to inspire faith in which everything is a test. One should rejoice in the good times and be patient in the bad times.

The trials that follow the coming of Prophets defy expectations since people expect great prosperity and a utopian environment. This shattered expectation is also reflected in the fact that the Prophets are only men. In Chapter 25 verse 20 it is stated that all Prophets were men in that they ate food and walked the streets. This is repeated in Chapter 17 verse 94. Ibn Kathir added in his explanation of this verse that Messengers are sent to their own people so that they will understand these Messengers. If an angel were sent to the people in general they would have nothing in common with the angel.

In Chapter 19 verses 35 to 37 the concept that the Prophets were only men is stressed regarding the Prophet Jesus. In these verses it is explained that God does not bear children, but creates only by declaring it to be. As Ibn Kathir explained God created Jesus as a Prophet and servant of God only.

In verse 37 it is explained that there developed various sects around the person of Jesus. As Ibn Kathir explained, some rejected him, some deified him and some designated him only as a Messenger and servant of God. The Qur'an clearly labels him as only a Messenger of God.

There is some proof for this belief in the Gospels themselves. In Matthew 23:8-10 Jesus states that there is only One Master. He was referring to God. In John 5:19 Jesus said that he can do nothing except by the Will of God. These two verses that reference Jesus as a servant of God and not His equal are confirmed in the verses in the Qur'an. It also personifies the perspective that Muhammad had regarding his relationship with God.

The idea that Jesus was a Prophet was confirmed in Matthew 21:46. In this verse the Pharisees were angry with Jesus for what he had said, but they feared that if they attacked him the people would rise up against them. The people largely understood that Jesus was a Prophet. This is verified in the story of the loaves of bread and fish in John 6:14 in which the people were awe-stricken by the multiplication of the bread and fish amongst the multitudes of people. They declared that he was a Prophet and in the next verse (15) Jesus had to leave because he perceived that the people aimed to make him a king which was not the mission of Jesus. The reaction of the people to make Jesus a king was in line with the expectations of the Israelites that the Messiah would be a warrior-king like David. As stated by the biblical scholar Bart Ehrman, "a great and powerful warrior-king, or an even more powerful cosmic judge of the earth – this is what some Jews expected of the Messiah."[69]

Instead, Jesus was sent to reinvigorate the faith of his people (Matthew 9:12; 10:5-6) which despite good knowledge of the Law was largely lost (Matthew 23:2-3). In Luke 11:30 Jesus clearly compared himself to Jonah in that he was a sign to his people as Jesus was at that time a sign to his people. Despite the specific people and specific time period in which Jesus was oriented the relevance of his message was connected to all the Prophets before his time. Jesus stated in John 14:6 that he had brought the way, the truth and the life (true life) in which no person at that time could achieve Heaven except through the teachings of Jesus. This assertion of preeminence can be found amongst all the Prophets of any age. They bring the truth and a rejection of the Prophet who brings the truth is tantamount to rejection of that truth which results in a loss of salvation. This was the claim of the Prophet Muhammad.

The Meccan verses of the Qur'an describe the Prophet Muhammad in various ways. He is described as a warner, a reminder, a Messenger to all mankind, an obedient servant of God and an unlettered person. In Chapter 53 verse 56 as well as in Chapter 38 verse 65 the fact that Muhammad was only a warner is emphasized. He was warning the people because the error of their beliefs and actions have dire consequences.

He is also a reminder as described in Chapter 88 verses 21 to 22. In verse 21 the Prophet was told to give admonition which according to Ibn Kathir is a reminder of their true purpose on this planet and the punishment for going astray. In verse 22 the Prophet was told that these are the only roles of the Prophethood because he was not sent as a dictator over men. He could only warn and remind people, the rest was up to them.

It is also stressed in Islam and can be found in the Meccan verses of the Qur'an that Muhammad was a Prophet that was sent to all mankind. In Chapter 25 verses 51 to 52 it states that if God had willed He would

69 Ehrman, B. D. (2009). *Jesus, Interrupted: Revealing the Hidden Contradictions in the Bible (and Why We Don't Know About Them)*. New York, NY: HarperOne. (p. 232).

have sent a Prophet to every center of population, but He chose a select few to deliver His message to mankind. Muhammad was the final Messenger sent and he was sent to all mankind, not only the Arabs.

The believers are told in verse 52 to strive against the unbelievers with this Qur'an. The point that can be taken from this verse is the necessity the believers in Islam have to preach this message. There will always be rigorous opposition to Islam, but the Muslims are told throughout the Qur'an to strive against this disbelief which is one of their prime purposes of existing in this life.

There are three places in the Meccan verses that make it clear that the Prophet did not invent this religion. The first two places involves the punishment that Muhammad would face if he had disobeyed His Lord and said what he was not commanded to say. In Chapter 72 verse 22 the Prophet was told to say that if he disobeyed God none could save him from God. Further in Chapter 69 verses 44 to 47 it gives details to what would have happened to the Prophet if he had disobeyed God. Verse 46 reads that God would have cut off the artery of his heart, basically killing him.

The other place that it dispels the idea that the Prophet was speaking falsehood about his status as a Prophet is in Chapter 29 verse 48. In this verse it is asserted that the Prophet was unlettered, i.e. he could not read. He never read a book or engaged in religious scholarship before he received the first revelation of the Qur'an. According to Ibn Kathir this was proof that Muhammad did not invent the Qur'an.

9.1.2. Words of God Cannot Be Changed

In Chapter 18 verse 27 the unchangeability of God's Word is emphasized in the Qur'an. Just as there was one religion initially, the Word of God is considered to be one and eternal without change. In Islam when someone attempts to change those words it is a great sin called *bid'a* (innovation). No matter what God's Words remained unchanged, undistorted and not misinterpreted amongst those committed to preserving them. The early Muslims were very conscientious of this and took great care to preserve them and memorize them. This is why memorizing the Qur'an in the Muslim world is considered a great deed.

In the Gospels the continuity of the Words of God is also stressed. In Luke 16:17 it is stated that it would be easier for the Heavens and Earth to pass away than to have one word of the Law to disappear. This is a very strong statement that verifies that the Words of God are not something to be taken lightly nor are they anything that are easily ignored or forgotten. In fact, this verse indicates that the Words of God have more permanence than the Heavens or the Earth.

Mark 7:8-9 separates the traditions of men from the Words / Commands of God. The traditions of various peoples across the world are mostly invented and change with the passing of time. These verses in the Gospels separate these man-made traditions from the actual Commands of God which are permanent and will last forever. In the teachings of Jesus there are several places where the traditions of the Pharisees were denounced by Jesus as conflicts with the actual Word and Commands of God. This is the purpose of Prophets. Prophets in the Israelite and Ishmaeli traditions come when these traditions have distorted the original message sent by God so badly that a renewed message is needed to set the people back on the right track. This was what Jesus brought and this was what Muhammad brought.

9.1.3. Believers

A reality regarding belief is explained in Chapter 56 verses 13 to 14. The closest believers, those who have a higher faith, are amongst the earlier generations. Those who surrounded the Prophet and their immediate successors are considered the earlier generations in Islam. The later generations will not be as close in belief as these people, but a few of them will be better than the others. The more time that passes the more faith is affected so that once this planet expires it is believed in Islam that there will not be a single Muslim.

In the Gospels the pre-eminence of the believers over those who do not believe can be found in Matthew 13:43. In this verse it is stated that the righteous will shine like the sun in the Hereafter while in verse 42 those who disobeyed God and were embroiled in iniquity will be in the great fire. This is contrasted to this life in John 15:19 in which the believers are hated in this world because they are not of this world.

The believers are considered the despised ones. This is an amazing dichotomy. In the next life the believers will be of those who shine like the sun while in this life they are considered the most despicable. In this life the unbelievers are considered admirable people while in the next life they will be cast down into the deepest fires of Hell.

The oppression of people of belief in this life fulfills the concept of the believers being hated in this life. In the United States Commission on International Religious Freedom 2014 report 38% of the countries listed at first tier (most oppressive to religious freedom) were countries that were attacking / oppressing Muslims. This includes Burma, China, Eritrea, Tajikistan, Turkmenistan and Uzbekistan. Sadly, three of those countries (Tajikistan, Turkmenistan and Uzbekistan) are Muslim-majority nations led by super-nationalist / communist governments. The list does not include recent developments in the Central African Republic in which the Muslims have been mostly 'cleansed' from the country following mob rioting which witnessed such atrocities as a pregnant Muslim woman being murdered and her fetus cut out.[70] The Muslims are also being 'cleansed' from Burma which featured as the number one religious freedom violator in the 2014 report.[71] It is also likely that the religious freedom violations of Muslims in this report are under-reported as there are allegations that USCIRF has an anti-Muslim bias. The treatment of a Muslim hired by its commissioners and management has resulted in a court case that has led to people resigning from the organization and calls to abolish the USCIRF.[72]

The empirical investigation of discrimination against Muslims in non-Muslim environments is rare, but an article in 2011 in the journal *Politics, Religion and Ideology* seemed to indicate that Muslims are not discriminated against more so than other religious minorities. The

---

[70] Larson, K. (2014, April 27). "1,300 Muslims leave C. African Republic capital." Retrieved April 27, 2014, from news.msn.com/world/1300-muslims-leave-c-african-republic-capital.

[71] *2014 Annual Report | United States Commission on International Religious Freedom.* (2014). Retrieved from United States Commission on International Religious Freedom website: www.uscirf.gov/reports-briefs/annual-report/2014-annual-report.

[72] Hurd, E. S. (2013, January 24). "Muslims Need Not Apply" | *Boston Review*. Retrieved from www.bostonreview.net/world/muslims-need-not-apply.

authors applied simple t-tests while controlling for very little and used a timeframe (1990–2002) when discrimination of Muslims was unlikely to be an issue. They also defined discrimination as only affecting the minority religion however laws such as the hijab-ban in France which the authors reference is not included as discrimination against Muslims because it supposedly applies to all religions even though it really only affects Muslims.[73] The authors apparently have drawn new conclusions in an updated version of the article including data on discrimination until 2008. They have found that discrimination against Muslims is more likely than other religious groups in Western non-Muslim countries.[74]

9.1.4. Life

In Chapter 90 verse 4 the reality that man was created in toil and struggle is made clear and to the point. The *tafsir* from Sayyid Qutb explains this verse in excellent detail. Man's struggle starts at birth when the mother bears him in pain and he struggles to survive thereafter. Later in life there are various ailments, some of them terminal. The eventual result after all of this toil is death and the deeds will be weighed to determine if the short-term affliction of this life is met with the long-term affliction of the Hereafter. This is why Muslims are incredibly resilient to disaster whether natural or man-made.[75]

This is not to say that, according to Islam, God constantly afflicts man with disaster. On the contrary, most of the trouble in this life is caused by men and their actions. In Chapter 30 verse 41 it is stated that mischief has appeared on land and sea because of the hands of men. Ibn Kathir in his explanation of this verse stated, "Whoever dis-

---

[73] Akbaba, Y., & Fox, J. (2011). "Religious Discrimination against Muslim Minorities in Christian Majority Countries: A Unique Case?" *Politics, Religion & Ideology*, *12*(4), 449-470.

[74] ——. (2015). Securitization of Islam and Religious Discrimination: Religious Minorities in Western Democracies, 1990–2008. *Comparative European Politics*, *13*, 175–197.

[75] Qutb, S. (2012, March 6). *In the Shade of the Qur'an – Fi Dhilal Al Qur'an Vol. 18*. Retrieved August 10, 2014, from www.holybooks.com/shade-quran-dhilal-quran-sayyid-qutb/

obeys God in the Earth has corrupted it, because the good condition of the Earth and the Heavens depends on obedience to God."[76] In this case the more justice there is the more there are good things occurring in this life. Natural disasters will continue to occur, but man-made disasters which are the most disruptive will decrease and lead to order in the Heavens and Earth.

The problem is that people are given to injustice and various vices. In Chapter 70 verses 19 to 34 there are a number of characteristics of mankind that are listed to make this point. In verses 19 to 20 mankind is described as impatient who frets when s/he is touched by evil. In verse 21 s/he is described as stingy with the good s/he has been given by God. Ibn Kathir added in explanation of these verses from a *hadith*, "The worst thing that can be in a man is greedy impatience and unrestrained cowardice."[77]

This section of verses in Chapter 70 verses from 22 to 34 then describes those who are not like those who are cowards, impatient, and stingy. They are those who pray regularly and on time, they give to the needy, they believe in the Last Day, they fear God, they are those who properly cover themselves except with those who they are allowed to reveal themselves, they are those who tell the truth and keep their promises, and they are those who give true testimonies and stand by them. These people are destined for Heaven.

In the Gospels this point is solidified in Luke 17:33. In this verse it states that those who seek to save their life in this life will eventually lose it. This is referring to decisions that only seek to promote one's life in the present realm, i.e. what we consider to be life today. Many people cheat each other and do all kinds of nefarious things simply for gain in this life. The believer is constantly focused on the next life and will do things that rationally do not make sense when preserving the present life is the primary concern. In this way the person will gain life, i.e. gain the next life in Heaven.

---

[76] Quran Tafsir Ibn Kathir - Home. (2010, March). Retrieved from www.qtafsir.com/.
[77] Ibid.

9.1.5. The Angels

One of God's creation is the angels. Besides being the tools for the implementation of God's plan they are also appointed for the purpose of recording man's actions and deeds. They are also appointed for protection which is a concept known amongst Christians as guardian angels. In the Gospels, Jesus told his disciples in Matthew 26:53 that if he wanted he could pray to God to ask for the angels to help him from his enemies. The angels are also reported to have helped the Muslims in the Battle of Badr, the first battle the Muslims were involved in against their Meccan enemies. This is reported in a Medinan chapter, Chapter 8 verse 11 in which the angels were commanded by God to support the Muslims in the battle. In the Meccan verses in Chapter 82 verses 10 to 12 the angels are described as protectors and recorders in which they are assigned to each person.

In Chapter 50 verses 17 to 18 the number of these angels per person is two with one on his right and one on his left. These two angels are recording everything he says and does for the purposes of later judgment. In the preceding verse in this chapter (16) it is made clear that God knows everything that passes through his soul in which He is closer to him than his jugular vein.

The presence of the angels and the knowledge of God about all things are meant to remind mankind that there is nothing that s/he does or says that will not be held against him/her on Judgment Day. The fear of God starts with realizing this and accepting that He has power over all things. Those who do not recognize these facts are usually dismissive of religion and any concept of final judgment.

9.1.6. God Is All-Knowing

In the Qur'an there are many names given to God. One of those names is *al-Alim* which means the All-Knowing. In Chapter 35 verse 38 He is described for the first time as the Knower of the unseen of both the Heavens and the Earth. This name also appears in later Medinan chapters as well. In the Gospels Jesus also referred to God as All-Knowing. In Matthew 10:29-31 Jesus noted that all the hairs on the head are known by God indicating that God knows everything.

9.1.7. Prophecy

In the Meccan verses there are three prophecies about the end times. In Chapter 27 verse 82 the coming of the beast is mentioned. Ibn Kathir added in his explanation of this verse that this beast will come when mankind becomes thoroughly corrupt and neglectful of the commands of God. The religion of God will become so twisted that it will no longer be the religion of God. After these things occur the beast will appear on Earth.

In his explanation of this verse Ibn Kathir pointed out several signs that will precede this event in which the beast will come from Mecca. In Islam there are ten signs for the end times. The first sign is the rising of the sun from the west, the second sign is the appearance of a great smoke, the third sign is the appearance of the beast, the fourth sign is the appearance of Yajuj and Majuj,[78] the fifth sign is the coming of Jesus, the sixth sign is the coming of the *Dajjal* (Christians call this entity the anti-Christ), the seventh sign is three separate events in which there will be massive cave ins (sinkholes) in the west, the east and in the Arabian peninsula, and the final sign will be a great fire that will originate in Yemen.

Some of these signs are mentioned individually elsewhere in the Qur'an. In Chapter 43 verse 61 the coming of Jesus as a sign of the Final Hour is mentioned. In Chapter 44 verse 10 the coming of the great smoke is mentioned. These predictions for the future are meant to inspire the believers to prepare for them so when they occur they are ready.

In the Gospels Jesus also had several prophecies about things that had not come to pass at his time. In Matthew 8:11-12 Jesus prophesized that the correct belief will spread from east to west while those

---

[78] For more information on Yajuj and Majuj see this source: www.islamawareness.net/ Yajuj/disbelivers.html.

who had been given the message through the ages will be complete disbelievers. Jesus in this verse was referring to the tribes of Israel. In this prophecy the people from around the world will hold the true mantle of faith that through the ages had been isolated to a select group of people predominantly.

Another prophecy of Jesus that appears several times in the Gospels is the claim that there will be many false prophets that will come after his time (Matthew 24:5; 24:11; 24:24; Mark 13:6). It is these references that Christians through the ages have used to claim Muhammad was a false prophet. Although these claims can be used to dismiss Muhammad, it should be noted that Jesus never claimed to be the final Messenger. Muhammad did in Chapter 33 verse 40 in which he is called the 'Seal of the Prophets.'

After the departure of Jesus there did arise many false messiahs / Prophets / Messengers. Some of the bigger names are Menahem ben Judah and Simon bar Kokhba. One of these false prophets actually appeared shortly before the death of Muhammad. The name of this person was Musaylima and he sent a letter to Muhammad trying to strike a compromise in authority with Muhammad. Muhammad wrote a letter in return to this person stating, "From Muhammad the Apostle of God to Musaylima the liar. Peace be upon him who follows the guidance. The earth is God's. He lets whom He will of His creatures (to) inherit it and the result is to the pious..."[79] After the death of the Prophet there was a war between the followers of Musaylima and the Muslims. Musaylima was killed by Wahshi, the slave who had killed Hamza, one of the uncles of the Prophet and a great companion, in the Battle of Uhud. Wahshi was hired by Hind the wife of Abu Sufyan, one of the most powerful men of Mecca and an avowed enemy of Islam until the conquest of Mecca by the Muslims. Musaylima was not the last of the false prophets, but he was the first in the Islamic era.

---

[79] Guillaume, A. (2002). *The Life of Muhammad* (M. Al-Saqqa, I. Al-Abyari, & A.H. Shalabi). New York, NY: Oxford University Press. (Original work published 1937). (p. 649).

9.2. The Explanations: The Qur'an

9.2.1. Only One Religion

The religion of Islam maintains that God delivered to mankind only one message which was sent to various Prophets throughout time. In addition it asserts that the differences between them are due to human errors over time in transmitting those messages across people and across times. Sometimes these messages were intentionally changed as well. This will be discussed later in this book.

In Chapter 10 verse 19 it asserts that mankind was one nation. According to Ibn Kathir the people were originally united under one religion. Later they differed amongst themselves which caused divisions. In this verse mankind is told that they would have been destroyed for this if God had not given them respite for a time period.

Sectarianism plagued all generations of mankind and in all communities. Amongst the People of Israel this was the case also as described in Chapter 7 verse 168. In this verse the breaking up of their community into sects appears to be a deliberate act of God. Some of those groups are described as righteous while some are described as sinners. The verse also states that these different groups were tested through adversity and prosperity to help them turn towards God.

One of the arguments against the concept that the different religions had a common message/origin is the different commands in each faith that were clearly not later inventions. One example is the observance of the Sabbath. One of the things that irked the Pharisees at the time of Jesus was his disregard for the Sabbath. In Chapter 16 verse 124 it is explained that the Sabbath was ordered by God to be strictly observed by the People of Israel because they, according to Ibn Kathir's interpretation of this verse, left the original holy day. According to Ibn Kathir this holy day had always been Friday. In this case the observance of the Sabbath is due to a previous error in their community which was made strict for them as a means of punishment. The story of the fishermen who were turned to apes for violating the Sabbath shows how serious following the strict rules of the Sabbath was for the early People of Israel.

9.2.2. The Qur'an

The Qur'an is considered the greatest miracle brought by the Prophet Muhammad with the permission of God. In Islam it is considered the literal Word of God. In Chapter 10 verse 37 it asserts that none could produce the Qur'an except God. This is sometimes placed as a challenge to those who say Muhammad invented it. The challenge is to produce a Qur'an like it.

This verse also adds that the Qur'an confirms the former revelations emphasizing the one religion and eternal Word of God concept emphasized previously. The continuity of the religion and message does not mean that each Prophet came in a similar fashion with a mirror image message. The context was always different necessitating special approaches which is the main thesis of this book.

Ibn Kathir added a point in his explanation of this verse. The Qur'an was sent to the Arabs who were very good at poetry and the Qur'an impressed them with its liturgical style. Moses was sent with great magic which impressed the Egyptians who were good at magic. Jesus was sent to a people who at that time were making advancements into medicine and treatments for ailments and his ability to heal people impressed them. In every age the Prophet was sent with what could impress the people.

Even though the Qur'an was sent in Arabic, the message contained therein was for all the nations and worlds. Chapter 68 verse 52 reads the Qur'an was sent to all the worlds. Worlds in this case refers to the world of mankind and the world of *jinn*s, the unseen creatures mentioned in previous chapters who also have the freedom of choice.

9.2.3. Pre-Destination

One of the principles of faith in Islam is the belief in pre-destination. This pre-destination applies to individuals and entire populations. There are several verses throughout the Qur'an and in particular in the Meccan verses that indicate that entire populations of people will be exterminated when their pre-destined time arrives. The ultimate pre-destined time for all the world will be the Day of Judgment.

In Chapter 20 verse 129 the punishment for disobedience to God is pre-ordained, so those who engage in sin are given respite for a period. In Chapter 15 verses 4 to 5 and Chapter 7 verse 34, it is stated that every people / population has a term appointed which cannot be advanced or delayed. As is known, nations rise and fall, but the Muslims are instructed here that this is not random but pre-ordained. No nation lasts forever.

In Chapter 17 verse 58 it adds that this destruction will occur before the Day of Judgment. There may also be some calamity that occurs to that nation that would disrupt it. Many verses already cited have indicated the divine purpose behind these calamities and destructions. Mankind sins, God tests them, and mankind may choose to right themselves before the eternal penalty which is Hellfire.

9.2.4. Differences Are Signs

In Islam racial and cultural diversity is a sign of God's Greatness in the diversity of His creation. Far from being a cause of communal discord, diversity is celebrated in Islam. In Chapter 35 verse 28 the various colors of creatures and people inspire awe of God in which those who have knowledge are those who fear God. Ibn Kathir explained that those who have knowledge are of three types. The pious servant knows God and His commands. The ignorant is the one who knows God, but not His commands. Lastly, the transgressor is the one who does not know God, but knows His commands.

The concept of diversity as one of God's Signs is repeated in Chapter 30 verse 22. In this verse the diversity in languages is added as a sign of God's Greatness. Ibn Kathir explained that this Greatness is reflected in His powers of creation in that no one is exactly the same. When mankind creates things in large quantities s/he strives for uniformity which is the limit of his/her creative ability. God is greater than any person in that His imagination is limitless.

9.2.5. Heavens Split out of Fear of God

In Chapter 42 verse 5 the Heavens which are a far greater creation than mankind are almost split because of the might of God. This greatness is so amazing that mankind cannot even comprehend it yet they arrogantly disregard God and His commands. Mankind is given this choice though. S/he can choose to worship other things other than God, follow his/her own rules and engage in outright injustice or worship God alone, follow His commands and enjoin the right and forbid the wrong. The wrong choice will result in more pain and fear than ever imagined.

9.2.6. The Jinns

The *jinn*s in Islam are another creation that pre-dates mankind. They also were endowed with the ability to choose between right and wrong. They are much more powerful than humans, but people through their creative and moral achievements have surpassed the *jinn*s as a civilization. Mankind was created as superior to *jinn*s as pointed out earlier to the chagrin of the Devil who is a *jinn*s in Islam. The *jinn*s interact with people in which they exist on another plane of existence in which they can see people, but they cannot be seen by them, usually.

These interactions are usually not good. The concept of possession in Islam is when a *jinn* attempts to invade the body of a human. They also suggest things to people through whispers and they always draw nearer to the one who strays from the remembrance of God. Some people who exhibit extraordinary power collude with these creatures.

In Islam the plan of God is communicated before its implementation. The *jinn*s are able to travel to the lower heavens and listen in on this plan so they can know what is going to happen before it does. Sometimes they share this information with their human allies. God is aware of these spies and in Chapter 72 verses 9 to 10 He sends fiery objects to intercept them in their listening to prevent them from doing so. These are called shooting stars which are space rocks that enter the atmosphere. In Islam they have a purpose as all things do.

These shooting star events occur according to Islam when something is going to happen that God does not want the *jinn*s to hear. Ibn Kathir explained that these things occur if there is a Prophet on the Earth or if God intends to advance His religion in one way or another. Since the *jinn*s are both righteous and unrighteous as mentioned in verse 11 of this chapter there are some that would try to derail the plan of God through their evil ways. The Devil is committed to this as mentioned earlier.

9.3. Summary

The Qur'an and the Gospels provide a number of explanations about the world, the hereafter, faith and the creation. In both the Qur'an and the Gospels it explains that the Prophets were sent to mankind and these people were only men who were subservient to God. Further, Jesus stated that he was sent to reinvigorate the faith of his people and that he was a sign to them specifically whereas in the Qur'an Muhammad is described as a Messenger to all mankind. In the Qur'an the Qur'an itself is described as being from God alone in which it confirms the former revelations and that it is for all the nations in the world.

The Gospels and the Qur'an make it clear that the Words of God cannot be changed in that they are as permanent as God Himself. In the Gospels it explicitly mentions the Law as impossible to be altered by anyone or anything. This constancy is also reinforced by the notion that there is only one religion in which mankind was one nation that separated into various sects out of their error or even as a punishment from God. This concept is specially mentioned in the Qur'an alone.

The idea that former nations were firmer believers than those today is stressed in the Qur'an. Further, the Gospels point out that in the Hereafter these believers will be exalted but in this life they are hated by a growing body of those who do not believe in God and His religion. Sadly, this trend is increasing even though the Qur'an mentions that God is so mighty that even the Heavens are on the verge of splitting due to His greatness.

The Gospels add that those who seek to save their life, i.e. those only focused on promoting themselves in the present life will lose their life in the next world. The Qur'an reinforces this concept by noting that life is full of struggles which should lead to mankind learning from these events and refocusing on the next life. Instead he becomes more unjust and given to vice while becoming more greedy and cowardly. In this sense he loses the life in the Hereafter as mentioned in the Gospels.

The Qur'an describes the differences in the world such as racial and cultural diversity as signs of God's greatness. Besides the seen creation, the unseen creation is also discussed in both the Qur'an and the Gospels. The angels are described in both messages as helpers of the Prophets and the believers. The Qur'an alone mentions the *jinn*s which are another unseen creation of God which has the ability to ascend to the lower heavens and listen in on the plan of God. God then pelts these eavesdroppers with shooting stars.

In both the Qur'an and the Gospels God is described as All-Knowing. In the Qur'an one aspect of this All-Encompassing knowledge is the knowledge of things that have not happened yet. This is known as pre-destination in which the punishment is pre-ordained in which nations rise and fall by the command of God. The Day of Judgment similarly is pre-ordained.

In the Gospels and the Qur'an there are several prophecies of things that have not happened yet. In the Qur'an there is a prediction of the coming of the beast, the second-coming of Jesus, and the coming of the Great Smoke. In the Gospels there is a prediction that faith in the true religion will spread from east to west while the Tribes of Israel will be complete disbelievers. In addition, the Gospels also points out that there will be many false prophets.

CHAPTER 10

CONTRADICTIONS

Contradictions

There are several teachings in the Gospels that contradict with the teachings in the Qur'an in the Meccan period and in general. These contradictions are at the heart of many of the polemics that exist between Muslims and Christians. It needs to be stated that the number of these contradictory teachings are few in comparison to all of the teachings that coincide between the Gospels and the Qur'an so far discussed in this book. At this point there are many teachings of Jesus that coincide with the teachings of Muhammad during the Meccan period. After the Meccan period there are also many teachings in the Medinan period that also coincide with the teachings of Jesus which will be discussed in a subsequent chapter. This chapter will explain these differences while providing a potential reason for the differences between these teachings. At this stage this can only be speculative since neither of these men are alive today to ask in detail.

10.1. Marriage

In Matthew 19:11-12 Jesus made a reference to the eunuchs as men who have committed themselves to God and stated that if the person has the faith then they should try to live this lifestyle. In essence, Jesus appears to be emphasizing a life without sex which is committed to God alone. It is unknown if this is the teaching that inspired Catholic priests and nuns to abstain from marriage, but it is certainly a point of contention given the controversy around Father Albert Cutie.[80]

---

[80] Cutié, A. (2011). *Dilemma: A priest's struggle with faith and love.* New York, NY: Celebra.

This concept is rejected in the Qur'an entirely. There is no reference to marriage in the Meccan verses of the Qur'an so at least in the initial period of Islam there was no conflict. In the Medinan verses there are several references with entire chapters dedicated to the relationship between men and women. In Chapter 24 verse 32 the Muslims are told to marry in which Ibn Kathir explained that this verse was a command to marry. In explaining this verse, Ibn Kathir cited a saying of the Prophet Muhammad in which he said, "O young men, whoever among you can afford to get married, let him marry, for it is more effective in lowering the gaze and protecting the private parts. Whoever cannot do that, then let him fast, for it is a protection for him."[81] In another saying cited by Ibn Kathir, Muhammad said, "Marry and have children, for I will be proud of you before the nations on the Day of Resurrection."[82] In both of these sayings and in this verse in the Qur'an it is obvious that marriage in Islam is encouraged and is seen as a dissuasion to many potential sins that occur amongst single men and women.

10.2. Divorce

It does not appear that Jesus forbade marriage instead he emphasized in the previous verse abstention. In Matthew 5:32 Jesus stated that those who divorce their wife unless she commits adultery in consequence causes her to commit adultery and vice versa. This is re-phrased in Matthew 19:9 and Mark 10:11-12. In essence, once married it is expected that the marriage remains unless one of the spouses, in particular the woman, commits adultery. Divorce is not accepted in the teachings of Jesus according to the Gospels. The fact that this point is made more than once throughout the Gospels emphasizes that importance of not getting divorced especially since adultery in Mosaic Law was punishable by death. See Deuteronomy 22:22 and Leviticus 20:10.

Paul, a later follower of Jesus, who is credited with the spread of Christianity in the Greek and Roman world, was known to have had a

---

81 Quran Tafsir Ibn Kathir - Home. (2010, March). Retrieved from www.qtafsir.com.
82 Ibid.

much more lenient view of divorce than that of Jesus as reported in the Gospels.[83] Many Catholic countries including Ireland and Italy had bans on the dissolution of marriages. These countries have since changed their laws, but their ban on divorce was based on these teachings in the Gospels.

The Qur'an has no ban on divorce. There is no mention on matters of marriage or divorce in the Meccan verses so as before there is no conflict with the early period of Islam. The Medinan verses, on the other hand, have an entire chapter dedicated to divorce. In Chapter 65 divorce is permitted only after a waiting period which expands and contracts depending on whether there has been sexual relations and if the woman is pregnant. In explanation of this waiting period Ibn Kathir included a story of Abd Allah b. Umar who was one of the companions of Muhammad. He divorced his wife while she was menstruating which angered Muhammad who ordered Abd Allah to remain with her until she had finished her menstruation and then wait till the next menstrual cycle of which when that was finished than he could divorce her. This would make the waiting period about 3 months unless she was pregnant in which the period would extend till after the baby was born.

During this waiting period the wife was expected to be housed with her husband with no sexual contact unless the two reconciled their differences. According to Ibn Kathir the point of the waiting period is to allow the husband and wife to work out their differences so that their marriage can potentially continue. If after that waiting period the two still have not reconciled their differences then the husband and wife can separate on good terms. All of these events are expected to occur under the watchful eye of witnesses in which it is recommended that there be two trustworthy witnesses in this chapter.

In this chapter not only is divorce permitted, but it is given rules to guide the process. This is radically different than the teachings of Jesus in which the only rule is that divorce is not permitted. If one divorces

---

[83] Eisenbaum, P. (2010). *Paul was not a Christian: The Original Message of a Misunderstood Apostle*. New York, NY: HarperOne.

his wife and remarries then he is committing adultery according to the teachings of Jesus as reported in the Gospel. Adultery is also punishable by death in Islam, albeit it is a ruling not found in the Qur'an. The accusation of adultery in Islam can only be determined through witnesses who have to actually see the act of adultery occurring unless they produce a false witness which is strongly condemned in the Qur'an. Adultery is a major crime in Islam, but not one that is committed when one divorces his wife and remarries. Quite the contrary, according to the rules of Islam one can actually divorce and remarry up to three separate times with the same person of which after the third time that person no longer is permitted to the same spouse unless she gets married to another person and then divorces him.

10.3. Resurrection and the Spouses in the Hereafter

In Matthew 22:30 Jesus said that when the believers will be resurrected in the Hereafter they will not marry or have spouses, but they will be like angels. This is rejected in the Qur'an. In Chapter 44 verse 54 it is stated that in the Hereafter the believers will be wed to black-eyed and fair-skinned females. Ibn Kathir explained that this will be in addition to wives that they will also be married to as well who will be untouched and who will be so beautiful as to be compared to sparkling gems. This conception in Islam is where the myth of the 72 virgins arose for those who die a martyr amongst non-Muslims. The concept is valid, but the number of women is not delineated anywhere in the Qur'an.

Many have attacked this concept in Islam although it is hard to understand the reason since these events occur on another plane of existence. It also needs to be stressed that things described in the Qur'an take on literal and symbolic meanings as it says in Chapter 3 verse 7 in which some verses are definitive / clear and some are metaphorical. It can almost be guaranteed that any verse that refers to the Hereafter is metaphorical. This is verified in Chapter 2 verse 25 in which the believers who enter Heaven will see fruit and recognize it from their days on Earth, but it is not the same. As explained by Ibn Kathir regarding this verse as reported in a *hadith* in which Sufyan al-

Thawri reported from al-A`mash, from Abu Thubyan, that Ibn `Abbas said, "Nothing in Paradise resembles anything in the life of this world, except in name."[84]

Given these assertions is it possible that Jesus saying that the believers will be like angels and the Qur'anic assertion that the believers will have many wives are simply comparisons to things that people know in this life and enjoy? Men enjoy the presence of women as well as the power and beauty of angels. Does this necessarily mean that these assertions are literal truths? One can only speculate on this matter. Needless to say the concepts draw upon emotions that are often times juxtaposed to the pain and suffering that one will experience in Hell. The positive emotions of the descriptions of life in Heaven versus the negative emotions of the descriptions of Hell particularly in the Qur'an are added incentives for believers to strive to be the best they can be so they will enter Heaven.

10.4. Fasting

Fasting is something that Islam and Christianity share in common. The issue is not whether fasting is a part of the two faiths. The contradiction is in Luke 5:34 and Matthew 9:15 in which Jesus told his disciples that they were not to fast so long as he was with them. They were told in these verses that once he had left them they were to fast, but not before this time.

In the Qur'an fasting was not made obligatory for the believers until the Medinan period so again this does not conflict with early Islam in Mecca. It was made obligatory during the month of *Ramadan* which was the month when the first revelations of the Qur'an came to Muhammad. This was codified in Chapter 2 verse 185. The contradiction between the teachings of Jesus as reported in the Gospels and the Qur'an is that fasting was made obligatory during the life of Muhammad and in the Gospels it was actually forbidden while Jesus was with them.

---

[84] Quran Tafsir Ibn Kathir, 2010, op.cit.

10.5. The Death of Jesus

In Matthew 20:17-19 Jesus revealed to his disciples that after they enter Jerusalem he would be betrayed and given to the chief priests of the city in which they would give him to the Romans who would kill him and on the third day he would rise again. This is the Passion story that has captivated modern Christians who celebrate it every Easter. This is one of the concepts that divided the later Christians and Jews who rejected the idea that the Messiah would be killed and reinforced their belief that Jesus was not who he said that he was at that time.

This is a concept that is also rejected in Islam. This is rejected in a Medinan chapter, Chapter 4 verse 157. It is stated that those who are confused regarding the departure of Jesus from this world argue that he has been killed, which is refuted in this verse. In contrast, the verse states that a crucifixion and murder had taken place and many people had thought it was Jesus, but it was not him.

Ibn Kathir explained this verse in that in Islamic traditions there was a meeting between Jesus and his disciples slightly before the event. This meeting is also depicted in the Qur'an in Chapter 5 and in the Gospels depicted as the Last Supper. What is not in the Qur'an or the Bible is a tradition in the *hadith* that Jesus appeared before them on this occasion and prophesized that they will disbelieve in him. He then offered up to one of them the opportunity to have God disguise him as Jesus allowing Jesus to depart to Heaven untouched. The youngest disciple, largely believed in Christian circles to be John Zebedee, volunteered and it was him that was crucified while appearing as Jesus. This might also help explain why the person who appeared as Jesus cried to God asking Him why He had forsaken him in Matthew 27:46, which is an odd statement for a Prophet of God and even stranger for a Son of God. This statement only appears in Matthew though.

10.6. Jesus Dies for Forgiveness of Sins

In Matthew 26:27 – 28 at the Last Supper Jesus claims in verse 28 that his blood will be shed for the forgiveness of sins. This is another concept in Christianity that is largely refuted in Islam and the Qur'an.

In Islam the idea that sins are a personal responsibility that can be forgiven or not by God through faith and action has been discussed in this book already under the concepts of responsibility for one's own deeds (pp. 114–115), repentance (pp. 123–124) and God's Mercy (pp. 60–61).

The dichotomy in Christianity between works and faith that was the focus of Paul's interpretation of the teachings of Jesus that became mainstream Christian orthodoxy is predicated on this concept that Jesus died for the sins of mankind so all one needs to do is have faith in him to be saved. Paul did not want the Gentiles who converted to Christianity to follow Jewish law which for him and many in orthodox Jewish circles was only for Jews.[85] The strange thing about this teaching of Paul is that the Gospel writer who wrote Matthew felt that those who believe in Jesus still must follow the Law and do good deeds.[86]

10.7. Jesus Is Son of God

In Matthew 16:16–17 in response to a question on the person of Jesus, Simon Peter responded that Jesus is the Son of God of which Jesus responded in such a manner that he appeared to approve of the answer in verse 17. In John where there are more references to Jesus being the Son of God than any other Gospel there are more overt indications. In John 1:18 it is clearly dictated that God has a Son. In John 1:34 it is stated that Jesus is the Son of God. In John 1:49 another disciple responded that Jesus is the Son of God because Jesus revealed to him something that had happened to him in the past of which Jesus was not present to see it.

This is another concept that is refuted in the Qur'an in more than one place directly. This was addressed earlier in this book in the section Criticism of God Bearing Children (pp. 95–96). In Islam, the concept of God bearing children is refuted as well as the Christian concept, not found in the 4 Gospels, of there being a trinity. This is found

---

85 Eisenbaum, 2010, op.cit.
86 Ehrman, B. D. (2009). *Jesus, interrupted: Revealing the hidden contradictions in the Bible (and why we don't know about them)*. New York, NY: HarperOne.

in Chapter 4 verse 171 in which the Christians are addressed directly and told not to say, 'Three'. In this verse the idea that God is One is confirmed in Islamic belief and any idea that God has layers or bears children is not accepted.

As a matter of fact the trinity is found in only one place. As noted by Ehrman (2009), "the only place in the entire New Testament where the doctrine of the Trinity is explicitly taught is in a passage that made it into the King James translation (1 John 5:7-8) but is not found in the vast majority of the Greek manuscripts of the New Testament."[87] Christian scholars have largely concluded that these verses were a later inclusion which led some such as Desiderius Erasmus (1466–1536) to publish the Bible without these verses included which caused a public outcry and in response the verses were reinserted back into the Bible.[88]

10.8. A Possible Reason for the Differences

The differences between Jesus and Muhammad inspired this book. Many books have been inspired by this in an effort to drive a wedge as deeply as possible between these two men in an effort to promote one religion over the other. As noted earlier, Christian authors have worked the hardest to drive this wedge since their theology is not inclusive of Islam or Muhammad. Some have been more divisive than others. This book is aiming to bridge this divide which really is the Muslim perspective regarding the messages and careers of Jesus and Muhammad. Less has been written from this perspective, sadly.

Many of these divisive books assume that Muhammad was a liar or even worse that he was possessed by the Devil. The crux of their concepts of the Qur'an is that it was appropriated material from various Christian sources, some orthodox and some considered heretical. Their proof for this is scant except finding nominal correlations in the message of the Qur'an and the exegeses of some of these communities. It

---

[87] Ibid. (p. 186)

[88] Ehrman, B. D. (2007). *Misquoting Jesus: The story behind who changed the Bible and why*. New York, NY: HarperSanFrancisco.

should be noted that the message of Jesus was only a continuance of the former messages of previous Prophets so the accusation that Muhammad simply carried over former messages could easily be assumed of Jesus. Jesus himself was literate and learned in the Law of the Israelites. This is the beliefs of the atheists.

Muhammad was not raised in this environment, nor was he learned in the Law or traditions and in addition he was not even literate. The invention of a religion especially one that claims connection to previous messages would require scholarship. Muhammad was a tradesmen who had contact with Christians and Jews but not in any intense fashion that would be required for any type of learning to occur. As discovered by later scholars in Islam, learning a religion and teaching it is a lifelong endeavor. Muhammad started receiving the Qur'an in his 40s and he died in his 60s. Jesus started preaching in his 30s and departed not long afterwards. Not much is known about Jesus before he started preaching while there are many details of Muhammad of which none of those details include Muhammad being schooled in the Law and books of former Prophets.

Since there has already been much written trying to prove Muhammad is false this will not be reworded here. Another perspective is that the times and places of the men of God were different therefore requiring slightly different messages. This is one of the Muslim perspectives, but causes problems when one considers the differences. Another Muslim perspective is that the differences between the two messages are due to the errors of transmission/translation and deliberate alterations.

Ehrman (2009) believed that of these early groups, "the group that won out did not represent the teachings of Jesus or of his apostles."[89] The group that won out which Ehrman (2009) is referring to is the common conception of Christian doctrine that is still followed today. As Ehrman (2009) observed, "within 300 years Jesus went from being a Jewish apocalyptic Prophet to being God himself, a member of the Trinity."[90] Books that were included in the Canon were only done if

---

[89] Ehrman, 2009, op.cit. (p. 215).
[90] Ibid. (p. 260).

they followed Church doctrine while many of the earliest versions of the Gospel found today are considered heretical to this doctrine.[91]

The authenticity of the Biblical text is not explored in this book, but the authenticity of the Qur'an is explored in this section. The critique that is often used against the Qur'an is that it has more than one variant reading (*qira'at*) which means having more than one recitation. In the Islamic world there are 10 recognized readings of the Qur'an which differ in where the verse stops, some vowel differences and differences in letters.[92]

In Islamic tradition the Qur'an was originally codified under the direction of Uthman, who was the third *Caliph* in Islam and one of the prominent companions of the Prophet Muhammad. Later, as the Qur'an spread around the Muslim world mostly by oral recitation different dialects led to different ways of reciting the Qur'an which led to the different readings that are known today. Originally, there were more types of readings, but a scholar in the 10th century was successful in reducing the number to 7 of which 3 more were added later.[93]

In addition, some historians have doubted the early canonization of the Qur'an because of inscriptions that they have found on the Dome of the Rock complex in Jerusalem which differ from the text in the Qur'an. As pointed out by Whelan (1998) these inscriptions were likely embellishments of the Qur'anic text akin to a sermon and not an exact reproduction of verses of the Qur'an.[94]

Whelan (1998) also noted that there appears to have been a developing trade in the early period of Medina not long after the death of Muhammad in which people copied the Qur'an. She bases this information on Muslim historical sources of which she added, "the details cited here are scattered almost at random through texts of different character and period, and the references are too peripheral to the main

[91] Ibid.

[92] Bewley, A. (n.d.). *The Seven Qira'at of the Qur'an.* Retrieved August 13, 2014, from www.iium.edu.my/deed/articles/qiraat.html.

[93] Ibid.

[94] Whelan, E. (1998). Forgotten Witness: Evidence for the Early Codification of the Qur'an. *Journal of the American Oriental Society, 118(1), 1-14.*

accounts and the individuals too insignificant to have been part of a conscious, however pious, forgery of early Islamic history concocted at the end of the eighth century."[95] A sustainable trade as a Qur'an copier would indicate that the Qur'an was codified early in which Whelan (1998) concludes that, "the Muslim tradition is reliable, at least in broad outline, in attributing the first codification of the Qur'anic text to Uthman and his appointed commission."[96]

This would indicate that the Qur'an was codified by eyewitnesses i.e. those who were the companions of the Prophet Muhammad. It was collected under the authority and consensus of the Muslim community and state and tested through its memorization by the people. This is something that was not done for the Bible. The authors of the different Gospels were not the disciples.

The different readings of the Qur'an do not lead to dramatically different interpretations and by most accounts are trivial. This was even the conclusion of those historians who have concluded that the Qur'an was not canonized until much later.[97] The differences still raised concern in the Muslim world which in contrast to Medieval Europe at this time encouraged Muslims to own books and recite the Qur'an regularly. The gaining of knowledge in Islam is considered a sacred duty enshrined in the first command given to Muhammad, read. In addition, the Qur'an refers to itself as a clear text in which it is a book meant to be read by all who believe in God, His commands and the Final Hour.

In contrast to scholarly traditions in Medieval Europe as well, the Muslim world was deeply concerned about maintaining the authenticity of the text more so than upholding dogmatic truths. As concluded by Whelan (1998), "it is clear that even in the Muslim tradition the fact was acknowledged that readings of the Qur'an continually diverged from a supposed original; it is clear also that steps had repeatedly to be taken to impose or protect a unitary text of revelation-in the time of Uthman, again in the time of Ibn Mujahid, and even as recent-

---

[95] Ibid. (p. 13).

[96] Ibid. (p. 13).

[97] Whelan, 1998, op.cit.

ly as the 1920s, when scholars at Al-Azhar prepared the currently most widely used edition."[98]

The argument here is not that the Qur'an is unsusceptible to alterations, but that the Muslims were much more aware of this fact and concerned about it than the early Christians were in Medieval Europe. During the Renaissance and the Enlightenment European Christians began to become more textually critical of the Bible, but by that time centuries had passed that could not undo potential problems with the text that had become ingrained in the imaginations of the people.

There have been efforts to uncover ancient Qur'ans to see if the Qur'an can be verified with its ancient forebears. As stated by Whelan (1998), "at present there is no convincing evidence for the survival of any Qur'an datable earlier than the ninth century."[99] At least this was true when Whelan wrote that article in the late 20th century. An exciting new find at Birmingham University in the United Kingdom of a Qur'an that radiocarbon dating can place at least as far back as 645AD, but possibly as early as 568AD, verifies that the Qur'an was not altered through the centuries. The Qur'an was part of the Mingana Collection which was collected by a Chaldean priest in the 1920s. The Qur'an written in the Hijazi script, an early form of written Arabic, was written by someone very likely alive at the time of the Prophet Muhammad and may have heard him preach.[100]

10.9. Summary

In this chapter the contradictions between the Gospels and the Qur'an are discussed in detail. Some of these contradictions are with Medinan verses since some of these issues were not covered during the Meccan period. One of these contradictions is regarding marriage in which the Gospels recommend trying to live without sex i.e. not getting married while in the Qur'an the Muslims are encouraged to get married.

---

[98] Ibid. (p. 3).

[99] Whelan, 1998, op.cit. (p. 114).

[100] Coughlan, S. (2015, July 22). 'Oldest' Koran fragments found in Birmingham University - BBC News. Retrieved from www.bbc.com/news/business-33436021

Another contradiction with a Medinan verse is the other side of the equation, divorce. The Gospels do not permit divorce unless the spouse, particularly the woman, commits adultery. In the Qur'an divorce is permitted, but there are rules that govern the divorce. The rules encourage reconciliation, but do not forbid divorce.

The Gospel assertion that Jesus died and was resurrected is refuted in a Medinan verse. In the Qur'an it is stated that it only appeared as if Jesus was murdered, but he was not. This account verifies that a crucifixion did happen and that people did think it was Jesus, but according to the Qur'an it was not Jesus.

Finally, the Medinan verse that commanded the Muslims to fast while the Prophet was amongst them contradicts the command by Jesus as recorded in the Gospels to not fast while he was amongst them. In the Qur'an fasting is commanded during the month of Ramadhan in honor of the first revelation of the Qur'an which occurred during this Hijri month. The followers of Jesus were only commanded to fast after Jesus departed them in which there is scant details on how to fast.

The other differences involve purely Meccan verses. One of these contradictions involves the hereafter and what will occur with the believers. In the Gospels it is stated that the believers will become like angels and will not have spouses. In the Qur'an it is stated that the believers will have spouses and in addition they will have black-eyed and fair-skinned females.

Another contradiction involves Jesus dying for the sins of others. The Gospels record that Jesus predicted before his crucifixion that his blood would be shed for the forgiveness of sins. In the Qur'an it is stated that everyone is responsible for their own sins in which they have to repent, seek God's Mercy and do good deeds so they outweigh the bad deeds.

A major contradiction is the Gospel assertion that Jesus is the literal Son of God. This concept was rejected early in the Meccan period primarily in a refutation of the beliefs of the pagan Arabs who believed the angels were the daughters of God. It is stated clearly in the Qur'an that God does not have a son or any other partner in which He is only One.

Finally, the possible reasons for these differences are explored in this chapter. One idea is that there were different contexts between Muhammad and Jesus although this was deemed highly unlikely given the very contradictory messages. The other reason was errors in translation/transmission or further deliberate alterations which were deemed highly likely given biblical scholarship on this subject.

CHAPTER 11

SIMILARITIES: BEYOND MECCA

Similarities: Beyond Mecca

There are many teachings of Jesus in the Gospels that resonate with the teachings of Islam that are found outside the Meccan verses of the Qur'an. These teachings are discussed in this chapter. In the previous chapters the themes from the first three years and the remaining ten years in Mecca guided the discussion. In this chapter and subsequent chapters the teachings of Jesus guide the discussion.

The point of this chapter is to show the level of similarity between the messages of Jesus and Muhammad. The previous chapter highlighted the contradictions in the messages. Some of these contradictions between the teachings of Jesus and the teachings of Muhammad were evident from the early years of Qur'anic revelation in Mecca. These contradictions are a smaller percentage of the total teachings of Jesus found in the Gospels although some of them are major differences.

In addition to those teachings of Jesus that appear in the teachings of Muhammad in Mecca there are other teachings of Jesus that can also be found in the Qur'an in Medina. The scope in this chapter is widened beyond the Meccan years to incorporate the Medinan years. Since this book is focused on the Meccan years these similarities are only discussed in this chapter.

11.1. Jesus Is the Servant of God

In Matthew 10:24 and John 13:16 Jesus used the analogy of the role of the servant in regards to the master. Jesus made it clear in these verses that the servant is not above the master. The master in the analogy is God while the servant is Jesus. The fact that Jesus referred to himself as a servant of God is a clear Islamic concept in which Muhammad described himself as a servant of God. Even though this concept was already a part of Islam in Mecca, the Medinan verses explore this concept as well.

A servant is not a deity worthy of worship. When a Prophet describes himself as a servant he is making it clear that he is subservient to the supreme power in the universe i.e. God. This helps to assuage confusion over the person of the Prophet who brings the message from God. In the Qur'an this is more clearly elucidated in Chapter 3 verse 144 which states that Muhammad is only a Prophet. Ibn Kathir explained this verse in that its revelation occurred after the defeat at the Battle of Uhud in the Medinan era when many Muslims were killed in battle. There was a rumor spread that the Prophet had been killed which caused dismay and disorder. This verse states that even if Muhammad was killed the message lives forever because it is God's Message and God is forever while Muhammad is only a Prophet who can and eventually did die of old age.

11.2. Jesus Explains the Son of God Reference Is Not Literal

There is an amazing exchange recorded in John 10:33-36 in which the Pharisees, the leaders of the Jewish community in Palestine, confronted Jesus and threatened to stone him for blasphemy. The accusation that Jesus committed blasphemy was due to their belief that Jesus was labeling himself God while amongst the ancient Jews as it was with the Muslims, there is only One God. Jesus responded that in their scriptures the concept of being labeled a 'god' is bestowed on those of whom came the Word of God.

This was the point established by Ehrman (2009) and Eisenbaum (2010).[101] If the ancient Jews were confused about Jesus' reference to himself as 'god' or the son of God then it can only be expected that later generations of Greeks with a thoroughly pagan past steeped in polytheism and concepts of god(s) having children to be equally if not more confused with the references of Jesus. Jesus was making the point

---

[101] Ehrman, B. D. (2009). *Jesus, interrupted: Revealing the hidden contradictions in the Bible (and why we don't know about them)*. New York, NY: HarperOne. & Eisenbaum, P. (2010). *Paul was not a Christian: The Original Message of a Misunderstood Apostle*. New York, NY: HarperOne.

in this exchange with the Pharisees that he meant that his reference was in the same frame as the reference in the former scriptures amongst the Jews in that he was simply indicating that he was close to God, like a son. The reference was not literal, but figurative.

This is an interesting exchange which gives credit to the Islamic concept that Jesus was only a Prophet and not a deity or a son of God. In the Qur'an there is an interesting exchange between Jesus and God foretold on the Day of Judgment when God will ask Jesus if he told his people to worship him and his mother, Mary, as gods besides God. Jesus will go on the defensive regarding this accusation because it is a serious crime to lie about God. Jesus will respond according to the Yusuf Ali translation of Chapter 5 verses 116 to 118,

> "Glory to Thee! Never could I say what I had no right (to say). Had I said such a thing, thou wouldst indeed have known it. Thou knowest what is in my heart, Thou I know not what is in Thine. For Thou knowest in full all that is hidden. Never said I to them aught except what Thou didst command me to say, to wit, 'worship Allah, my Lord and your Lord'; and I was a witness over them whilst I dwelt amongst them; when Thou didst take me up Thou wast the Watcher over them, and Thou art a witness to all things. If Thou dost punish them, they are Thy servant: If Thou dost forgive them, Thou art the Exalted in power, the Wise."[102]

In this response to God's inquiry into what Jesus told his followers Jesus will tell God that God knows what is in his heart and that he only told them what God had commanded him to say to his people. Jesus will repeat this command to worship God who is both his God and the God of his people. Lastly, Jesus will make a prayer to God to forgive his people for their errors which will depend on His Mercy.

11.3. Sins That Are Not Forgiven

In Matthew 12:32 and again in Luke 12:10 and Mark 3:28-29 Jesus stated that those who speak against him will be forgiven but for those that speak against (blaspheme) the Holy Ghost will not be forgiven by

---

[102] Ali, A. Y. (2010). *The Meaning of the Glorious Qur'an*. Istanbul, Turkey: ASIR Media. (p. 82 – 83).

God. In Christianity the Holy Ghost is an ambiguous entity. In Islam the Holy Ghost is known as *al-Ruh* (The Spirit) and it is associated with the messenger angel i.e. Gabriel. Gabriel is the angel who brings messages from God to the Prophets. The injunction by Jesus to not blaspheme the Holy Ghost could be an indirect method of saying that one should not blaspheme against God. This calls into question the reason why Jesus explicitly stated the Holy Ghost and not God. This also calls into question the translation. This will be addressed later.

In Islam there is also a sin that is not forgiven similar to what Jesus expressed in the verses above. In Chapter 4 verse 116 it is stated that all sins could be forgiven by God except the sin of worshipping other gods beside God. This would be blasphemy towards God which may or may not be covered by the statement made by Jesus highlighted above. In Islam, the sin of polytheism or worshipping another god besides God is so serious that even the sin of murder could be forgiven by God, but not this.

11.4. Love Jesus more than Family

In Matthew 10:37 it is stated that anyone who loves their father or mother more than Jesus will not be worthy of him i.e. Jesus. This statement also includes sons and daughters as well. The love for the Prophet in Islam is also stressed similar to this statement of Jesus. In Chapter 33 verse 6 it is stated that the Prophet is more worthy of the believers than even their own selves. This is more intimate to the person than even the parents or off-spring.

Ibn Kathir highlighted a *hadith* in which the believer does not truly believe until the Prophet is dearer to him/her than his/her wealth, children, his/her own self and all the people in the world. This is a sweeping statement that is also seemingly captured in the words of Jesus above. Ibn Kathir also reported a story in relation to this verse about the prominent companion Umar. One day the Prophet asked Umar if he loves him more than all things including himself. Umar verified that he loved him more than all things except himself. The Prophet is reported to have responded to Umar by saying, "Oh Umar, your faith will never be complete until you love me more than yourself."[103] After this Umar did some self-reflection and returned and told the Prophet that he loved him more than himself. Later in this story Umar explained what happened in his self-reflection. He is reported to have said that he thought deeply about who he needed, himself or the Prophet and he concluded he needed the Prophet more.

The love for the Prophets is why Muslims get so upset when someone mocks the Prophet Muhammad in cartoons, etc. The level of anger is never understood in the non-Muslim world which often parodies Jesus in cartoons and stories without much reaction from Christian communities. In this verse in the Bible Jesus informed the believers that he is to be loved more than even the parents or children. Is Jesus loved more than the families of people who supposedly follow him? Can the same be said about the Muslims in today's world? What if people were to insult one's son or mother in the same way that people insult Jesus or Muhammad? Would the reaction be the same from this person?

11.5. The Powers of Jesus

In Matthew 9:6-8 Jesus healed someone who had palsy. The people who saw it praised God and it is stated clearly that this power of God was given to a man, i.e. Jesus. This is an important point that is also confirmed in the Qur'an. In Islam, the powers of Jesus are believed to have been from God alone, not from Jesus.

In Chapter 5 verse 110 it is stated that Jesus was given certain powers such as causing life where none existed and healing the blind and lepers. It states after each of these powers are pointed out that these powers were given to Jesus by God's leave, i.e. His permission. Ibn Kathir explained that these powers, miracles and extraordinary acts were granted to Jesus by God's leave, power and will.

The point that is made in the verses in the Gospels above and the verse in the Qur'an in Chapter 5 is that all the powers given to the Prophets such as the power to heal to Jesus, the power to separate the sea by Moses and the power to split the moon by Muhammad are not

---

[103] Quran Tafsir Ibn Kathir - Home. (2010, March). Retrieved from www.qtafsir.com/.

powers that these men possessed themselves. They were given these powers by God who is the only one who has the power to do any of these things. In extension, in Islam anything a man/woman does is by the leave of God which includes things that most people take for granted such as breathing.

11.6. Jesus as Judge

In Matthew 25:31-32 Jesus was predicting while under trial by the Romans and Pharisees that at the end times the nations of man will be gathered in which Jesus will separate them. This implies that Jesus will judge the nations based on some criteria separating them into good and bad. In Islam, the role of any Prophet in judging nations in this manner is rejected, but the concept of the Prophets acting as intercessors is accepted. As an intercessor a Prophet will act as a middle man between God and the people in which God will listen to the arguments of the Prophets on behalf of their people before casting final judgment upon them. This was highlighted above in the words of Jesus in the Qur'an when Jesus will ask God to forgive his people. In Islam the ultimate intercessor will be Muhammad as the final Messenger of God.

In addition, the idea that the Prophets are judges is something that is also confirmed in the Qur'an and the teachings in Islam. In Chapter 4 verse 65 it is stated that the faith of a people is incomplete until the Prophet is made as a judge between them and the decisions rendered from his judgment are fully accepted. Ibn Kathir explained that there were two stories that this verse may have been revealed about at the time of the Prophet in Medina. One is a story about a dispute over water for irrigation and another regarding two people in a dispute over an unknown issue. In both cases, the ruling of the Prophet took precedence in which in both stories the person who felt wronged by the decision was criticized for not accepting the ruling of the Prophet.

The Prophet Muhammad was considered among other titles the chief judge of the city-state of Medina. He only arbitrated issues involving the Muslim community and allowed the other religious community, i.e. the Jewish community to arbitrate over their own affairs. This did not mean that some Jewish community members did not rely on the Prophet for fair and unbiased judgment. In Islam, justice is something that is emphasized as it was early on in the Meccan years as established earlier in this book in the section 'Fairness and Justice' on pages 119 to 122.

The legacy of the judge in Islam established by the Prophet Muhammad carried forward into Muslim administration centuries later. For instance, in the Ottoman Empire a *Qadi* or judge was one of three core members of the Ottoman administration of cities across its empire.[104] Even in a place as tumultuous as Somalia, the Islamic Courts Union was established which was a consortium of Islamic judicial systems. It united Mogadishu for the first time in 16 years and established peace and security for the first time in Somalia since the beginning of the civil war. Ethiopia invaded Somalia and disbanded the Union which interestingly led to the formation of al Shabab, the Somali terrorist group.[105]

11.7. Jesus Brings New Teachings

In the Gospels Jesus made an analogy about new cloth and an old garment. He also made an analogy about new wine in old bottles. He noted in Matthew 9:16-17 that they cannot be combined i.e. new cloth with old garments or new wine with old bottles. The new cloth requires new garments and the new wine requires new bottles. This analogy is directed at the message that Jesus brought to his people at that time. The message was new. It was not entirely new as Jesus confirmed the Law before as has been established already, but there were new teachings of Jesus that broke with some of the teachings of the previous Messengers.

This is highlighted as one of the potential reasons for the mismatch between the messages of Jesus and Muhammad in the previous chapter. Although there are some things that Jesus supposedly said in the Gospels that were not confirmed by any Prophet before Jesus or by the

---

[104] Fritschy, W. (2008). *Indirect Taxes and Public Debt in 'the World of Islam' before 1800*. In S. Cavaciocchi (Ed.), *Fiscal Systems in the European Economy from the 13th to the 18th Century, 51-74*. Firenze: Firenze University Press.

[105] Ngugi, M. W. (2013, October 4). *How al-Shabaab was born | World news | theguardian.com*. Retrieved from www.theguardian.com/world/2013/oct/04/kenya-westgate-mall-attacks.

Prophet Muhammad which causes some concern regarding the rendition of this message as we have it today. The analogy in these verses helps to establish the incidence of abrogation.

In Chapter 2 verse 106 in the Qur'an it is stated that God causes some verses to be abrogated or forgotten in which they are replaced by something that is better or equal to those verses that are replaced. In Arabic the term abrogation is *nasikh*. The issue of abrogation in the Qur'an is contentious. As stated earlier, some believe including Muslims who take free license to attack non-Muslims or other Muslims that the verses in the Meccan era were abrogated by later verses in the Medinan era that called for the Muslims to fight. It needs to be stated that this is not the case. As stated by Zakaria Bashier, who received his Ph.D. in Islamic Philosophy from the University of Pittsburgh and is the Vice Chancellor of the University of Juba in Sudan, "the mild verses revealed before the verses of the sword could be viewed as alternative policies and strategies that continue to be valid and which are to be practiced should the circumstances require a less militant handling than the verse of the sword."[106]

New circumstances require new teachings. This is the crux of the statement by Jesus and it is confirmed in the Qur'an. As stated by Bashier (2007), "the murdering of Zachariah and his son John, and the attempt on the life of Jesus by the forces of evil amply showed, I think, that changing times and human conditions both demanded and called for the resumption of the Prophet-warrior tradition of Judaism."[107] After all, as expected by the Jewish community in Palestine at the time of Jesus, the rejection of a messiah who was murdered without even a fight was one of the causes of the rejection of Jesus as the messiah.

As explained by Ibn Kathir regarding this verse in the Qur'an abrogation can either be replacing words with other words or replacing commands with other commands. The second of these embodies the largest change. Ibn Kathir also explained that this verse was in refutation to some people in the Jewish community in Medina who criticized

---

[106] Bashier, Z. (2007). *War and peace in the life of the Prophet Muhammad (peace be upon him)*. Leicestershire: The Islamic Foundation. (p. 26).
[107] Ibid. (p. 33).

rulings in Islam that differed from the rulings in the Torah. This verse explains that God does this and the teachings of Jesus in the verses described above in the Gospels also indicate that abrogation is something that occurred with both Jesus and Muhammad.

11.8. Fasting and Showing Off

Fasting was prescribed for the followers of Jesus after Jesus departed them in Matthew 9:15. One of the critiques Jesus had of the Pharisees was that they did many of their religious observances for show in order to gain respect in the community. It is hard to imagine this today where religious practice is actually shunned in such a way that any public observance of it is frowned upon in the non-Muslim world. In the Muslim world in some countries there is still respect given to religious practice so the problem of observing religion in order to gain respect is still an issue there. In Matthew 6:16 Jesus criticized those who fast and twist their faces while they fast so that others know that they are fasting in order to get attention and respect.

This practice is also scorned in Islam. In a *hadith qudsi* reported by Abu Hurayrah which can be found in the collections of Bukhari and Muslim, God tells the believers that all deeds that they do are for themselves except fasting which is for God alone. In this *hadith* the believer experiences two joys through fasting, the joy of breaking the fast and the joy of receiving the reward from God in the Hereafter for fasting. The idea that fasting is for God alone indicates that only God knows about or should know about it. If someone is intentionally disfiguring their faces to let others know he is fasting then the fasting is no longer for God alone which negates the purpose of fasting in Islam.

11.9. Offer Greeting of Peace before Entering Home

There are numerous etiquettes clearly stated in the Qur'an and traditions of the Prophet Muhammad. There are so many in fact that some followers structure their entire existence around the daily practices of the Prophet which includes such mundane things as how many times someone drinks from a glass of water at any one time. The Prophet habitually drank three separate times before he sat the glass back down.

In the Gospels these types of etiquettes are difficult to find. One etiquette is the injunction to greet someone in a house before entering it which can be found in Matthew 10:12. It is not a surprise that this advice by Jesus to his followers has a parallel in Islam. In Chapter 24 verse 61 the believers are told to offer the Islamic greeting of '*as-Salamu Alaykum*' which means 'Peace be upon you' before entering a house. Ibn Kathir explained that this is obligatory in Islam.

In Islam depending on the building that is being entered there are different types of greetings. There is a special greeting for the mosque, a special greeting for one's own house and a special greeting for an empty house. At the core of all of these greetings is the word '*Salam*' or peace.

11.10. Loving Your Neighbor

The importance of maintaining neighborly relations in Christianity and Islam is paramount for the believer. In Matthew 22:39 Jesus was reporting the important commandments of which one of the most important is loving your neighbor as you love yourself. This is repeated in Mark 12:31. In reporting this commandment as one of the most important for the believers to obey Jesus was stressing the importance of maintaining good relations with one's neighbor.

This concept has a direct parallel in Islam. The concept is found in the *hadith* which is reported in the *Sunan* of Ibn Majah and *Musnad* of Ibn Hanbal. The first tradition reports that the Prophet told the believers to love for others what they love for themselves. The second tradition reports that the Prophet also told the believers that they do not truly believe if their neighbors are not safe from their abuse. These two statements are incredibly important in Islam towards Muslims establishing good relations with their neighbors.

11.11. The Public Servant

In one of the best verses in the Gospels, Jesus stated in Mark 10:42-45 that the believers will be different in how they rule over each other.

Unlike the non-believers who exercise authority over each other from the greater to the lesser, amongst the believers the lesser will be greater. In this sense, a leader amongst the believers will actually be a servant not a ruler in the sense of the word. This might be one of the earliest concepts of public servitude in which the people in government exist to serve the public, not the other way around.

In the life of the Prophet Muhammad this idea was embodied by how he administered Medina. Unlike Jesus, Muhammad actually had the privilege in running a government so he literally could practice what he preached. In a well-known *hadith* Muhammad was found sleeping on a mat on the floor with very little to eat in the storeroom of his house. This was his condition despite being the ruler of Medina with access to as many riches as he could gather from the people. Umar became so upset about the condition in which he found Muhammad that he exclaimed that Muhammad should live as the rulers of Rome and Persia in which Muhammad replied that the next life is much better than this life.

Muhammad was known to have paid the debts of those who passed away in Medina. And even though 1/5 of the war booty that was designated to the Prophet came to him after the different expeditions he used little of it for his family and spent the rest on the community and its defense. He was known to give away any wealth that came to him. He did this so frequently in fact that many of Muhammad's followers including the illustrious Umar made it a point of his administration of the *Caliphate* that the various governors of the Islamic world would not be allowed to accumulate wealth.

11.12. Testimony of Two Men

In John 8:17 Jesus brought up Mosaic Law regarding the required number of men for a testimony. In this tradition the required number of men is two. In the Qur'an this is also something that is addressed. In Chapter 2 verse 282 the required number of male witnesses needed for a loan contract is two. In this verse these witnesses are required to give testimony if there are problems between the loaner and the debtor.

Ibn Kathir explained this section of this verse in that this requirement is for contracts that involve money. There are other circumstances that require a different number of witnesses such as in a marriage contract or when accusing someone of a crime. As mentioned in the verse, for immediate transactions such as buying and selling this is not required, but for contracts that involve the transfer of funds this is required.

11.13. Eyes as a Source of Good / Evil

In the Gospels Jesus described the eye as the source of good / evil in a person in Matthew 6:22-23. In verse 23 in particular Jesus said that if the eye is evil then the whole body will be full of darkness. It can only be implied from this verse as well as other verses about the various body parts described by Jesus that when the eye is evil it looks at evil things thus making the soul evil.

In the Qur'an a body part is also singled out for the source of evil and good for a person. It is not the eye in the Qur'an that is the source of good / evil, it is the heart. In Chapter 22 verse 46 the eyes are directly referenced in that they are not necessarily blind, but the heart is blind. In Islam, the heart is the center of the person. If the heart is corrupted the person is corrupted much like what Jesus described for the eye. It can easily be linked since a person who has an evil heart will look at evil things thus further corrupting the person.

Ibn Kathir further explained this verse by stressing the importance of the heart in Islam. He included a wise saying in his explanation in that, "Ibn Abi al-Dunya said in his book *al-Tafakkur wa-l'tibar*, 'Some of the wise people said, 'Give life to your heart with lessons, illuminate it with thought, ill it with asceticism, strengthen it with certain faith, remind it of its mortality, make it aware of the calamities of this world, warn it of the disasters that life may bring, show it how things may suddenly change with the passing of days, tell it the stories of the people of the past, and remind it what happened to those who came before."[108] In this advice reproduced by Ibn Kathir the heart is the center for all instruction because of the impact the heart has on the actions of a person.

---

[108] Qur'an Tafsir Ibn Kathir, 2010, op.cit.

11.14. Martyrdom

In Matthew 16:25 Jesus explained that those who lose their lives for the sake of Jesus will find it, i.e. the true life will be revealed to them. This is repeated in Mark 8:35, although in Mark for the sake of the Gospels is also added and it is clearly stated that they will save their life. In Chapter 2 verse 154 in the Qur'an it is stated that those who are killed in the way of God are not really dead, but are living. This is a very comparable message to that of Jesus in the verses above.

11.15. Summary

This chapter explored areas of further concordance between the Gospels and the Qur'an in which the Medinan period of revelation is focused on in this discussion. The previous chapter included verses from the Medinan era to explain contradictions between the Qur'an and the Gospels. This chapter balances the equation by focusing on Medinan verses that have counterparts in the Gospels.

Jesus described himself in the Gospels as a servant of God while Muhammad is also described as a servant of God in the Qur'an. This concept of servitude which is characteristic of Prophethood further confirms the Qur'anic assertion that Jesus was only a Prophet while Jesus in his exchanges with the Pharisees also made a stunning comment that his reference to his divinity is not literal, but based on the Hebrew understanding that he has the 'Word of God' with him.

In the Gospels Jesus indicated that those who speak against the Holy Ghost will not be forgiven for this blasphemy. This is the only sin which Jesus stated was not forgivable by God. In the Qur'an it is stated that all sins can be forgiven by God except the sin of polytheism. At first glance these statements do not appear to be similar, but if one views the Holy Ghost as a part of the deity as it is in Christianity or as a messenger angel as it is in Islam than it can be boiled down to any blasphemy made against God is not forgiven by Him.

Jesus stated in the Gospels that to be a true believer s/he must love him (Jesus) more than they love their own father and mother. A similar assertion is made in the teachings of Islam in which love for

Muhammad must be so strong that they love him (Muhammad) more than they love even themselves. In either case it is clear that this love for the Prophets must be stronger than love for anything else.

In both the Qur'an and the Gospels the powers of Jesus are accepted as a fact. In particular, the power of Jesus to heal is confirmed in both of these messages. A further clarity is made in the Qur'an in which these powers were really not his, but they were the powers given to him by God. This is a point that is not made anywhere in the Gospels leading some to believe that these powers were from Jesus alone.

In both messages it is understood that the Prophets and in particular Jesus and Muhammad are considered to be the highest of judges. It is stated in the Gospels that Jesus will be the grand judge over the nations which is a concept that is rejected in Islam since it will be God who will be the judge. Despite this, the idea that these men possess the authority to judge is further confirmed in the Qur'an as well regarding the Prophet Muhammad. Unlike Jesus, Muhammad actually held the mantle of power in the city-state of Medina where he fulfilled various roles including judge.

The concept of bringing new teachings that did not exist in the previous messages is confirmed in these messages. In the Gospels Jesus made an analogy of new wine in old bottles as being incompatible with each other. The new wine was the new teachings brought by Jesus while the old bottles were the messages the existed previous to them. In the Qur'an, the concept of abrogation has a similar meaning in that former messages sometimes are abrogated, forgotten or replaced by something either equal or better.

In both messages it is recommended that when a believer is fasting these individuals should not show off since fasting is something that is for God alone. In both messages, it is also recommended that when entering a home the salutation of peace should be made before entering it. In addition, these messages also command the believers to love their neighbors as they love themselves.

Jesus stated in the Gospels that the leader is actually the servant of the people. Although Jesus never had a chance to lead his people, Muhammad did have this chance and he lived this command in his daily practices in Medina. The fact that Muhammad passed away with very few possessions despite being the leader of what would become the greatest empire founded on faith in human history indicates his charitable spirit.

Finally, both messages indicate that two men are needed for testimony in which the Qur'an further differentiates based on different types of testimony in which in Islam this is specifically for a loan contract. The Gospels, like the Qur'an further identify a single body part as being the source of evil in a person. The Gospels identify the eye while the Qur'an identifies the heart. These body parts have similar central functions in that the eyes look at evil while the heart inclines them towards it. Lastly, both the Qur'an and the Gospels explain that those who are killed in the way of God are not really dead, but they are living the true life which is the life in the hereafter.

CHAPTER 12

MUHAMMAD IN THE GOSPELS

Muhammad in the Gospels

There are a few places in the Gospels that signal to a Muslim reader that Jesus was predicting the coming of Muhammad. This is important because in the Qur'an it is stated in Chapter 7 verse 157 that the Prophet Muhammad is described in the Torah and the Gospels. This is repeated in Chapter 10 verse 94 that Muhammad is certainly mentioned in the scriptures of the Gospels and Torah, but it is either distorted or hidden.

This is one of the underlying assumptions that is rooted in the Muslim conceptions of revealed religion. The One God sent Prophets with a singular message potentially different but not substantially different to lead mankind to worship the one true God, the only one that truly exists in the universe. These Prophets foretold the coming of each other through the messages that God gave them. God is fully aware of all of the events that will transpire and He has prepared a succession of Prophets to provide proper guidance to mankind before their eventual doom. God lives in a place where time does not mean the same thing as time on earth. This is verified in the Qur'an when in Chapter 22 verse 47 it is stated that a day to God is like a 1000 years on the earth. God can see the past, present and future where these terms really only have meaning to people on earth. In God's terms it is very likely that the doom of the planet has already happened. This is something that perplexed Christians and Muslims because they were intently waiting for this event. Both Jesus and Muhammad indicated that it was very close.

The idea that another Prophet was coming after the coming of the Messiah i.e. Jesus seemed to be something that not only Jesus was possibly aware of, but the general population seemed to know about it. For instance, in John 7:40-41 there was an exchange amongst the people speculating over who was Jesus. Some of them said that he was the Prophet (the word Prophet is capitalized in the King James Version as well as other versions of the Bible) while others said that he was the

Christ. The people separated the two as if to say that there were these two separate entities that people were expecting. The only other Prophet could be John, but it is unlikely the people were confused on whether Jesus was John especially since John was imprisoned and later killed while Jesus was preaching the Gospel.

Besides this reality for Muslims that the Prophets were fully aware of each other and predicted each other, Muslims also believe that the message was practically the same and those who followed these Prophets can be aptly called Muslims as well. This has been the main argument of this book. Chapter 28 verses 52 to 53 state that those before the revelation of the Qur'an believed in the revelations that were sent them and when they hear the verses in the Qur'an they confirm its truth and in addition confirm that they were already Muslims. This concept has caused controversy with Christians because they refute a claim that the early Christians were in fact Muslims because this is a term used by the followers of Muhammad. The point is not the semantics of a particular language whether Greek or Arab, the point is the conception of those terms and whether that conception resonates between the teachings of these two men. A Muslim, in Islamic tradition is 'one who submits himself to God'. This concept is not alien to any followers of any Prophet, in fact, they all submitted to the Will of God.

In this case the differences between Islam and Christianity cannot be because Jesus and Muhammad believed in something the other did not. The differences, as stated earlier, must be because of the errors of mankind, intentional or not. In fact, when Muslims read this statement of Jesus in Matthew 7:22-23 in which he stated that at the end of time people will approach Jesus and say that they prophesized in his name, cast out devils and did many wonderful things in which Jesus will say that he did not know them and will ask them to leave his presence, Muslims imagine that Jesus was predicting the error that these people will insert into his community. In particular, Muslims would identify this statement as a direct affront to the assertions of Paul in which his epistles / letters to the various Christian communities in the Greco-Roman world actually pre-date the manuscripts that have become the Gospels today (Matthew, Mark, Luke and John).[109]

---

[109] Ehrman, B. D. (2009). *Jesus, interrupted: Revealing the hidden contradictions in the Bible (and why we don't know about them)*. New York, NY: HarperOne.

Paul was not a disciple of Jesus. He came later after Jesus departed the world. Supposedly, he had an inspiration in the famous 'road to Damascus' where Jesus appeared to him and he embraced the Christian message. Paul was deeply committed to spreading this message in which Paul referred to Jesus as lord. This message was designed for people who fully accepted polytheism i.e. the Greeks in which the goal was conversion not maintaining the authenticity of the original message if this message was even known by the time Paul was writing these epistles in the 50s AD. This has caused many Muslims to accuse Paul of being a major exponent of this concept. His message became the center-piece of Christianity in Europe and the Near East.

For instance, the Gospel of John was the last of the Gospels to be written. The Gospel of John is also the most cited of the Gospels amongst contemporary Christians because it codifies the later beliefs of Christians about Jesus such as he pre-existed, he is divine and on earth he became human. These assertions are not found anywhere in the previously written Gospels.[110] Despite these issues, the Gospel of John contains some interesting indications of a possible prediction of another Prophet to come after Jesus. These verses are only found in John.

In John 16:12-15 Jesus was telling his disciples that there were many things that he needed to tell them but they could not bear them at that time. Jesus then informed them that the Spirit of Truth will guide them in which he will not speak on his own behalf, but will communicate only what is communicated to him. This is a characteristic of Prophethood in that Prophets only say what God tells them to say in which they are not permitted to interject their own opinions into conveying that message.

There are two things of importance in these verses. The first important idea is that Jesus is holding back information because the community of believers at that time could not handle it. This is a characteristic of the contextual aspect of revealed religion. This supports the ideas that have been discussed in this book that the careers of Jesus and Muhammad are different in that only the contexts were different leading to additional teachings that Jesus did not convey to his community. Muham-

---

[110] Ibid.

mad never stated that the religion he brought was incomplete. Quite the contrary, in Chapter 5 verse 3 it is stated that the religion of Islam has been perfected and approved for the believers. This part of this verse was part of the Last Sermon of the Prophet and is widely believed to be the last revelation of the Qur'an before the death of Muhammad.

The second important idea is that Jesus was clearly stating that someone whom he described as the Spirit of Truth will come to tell his community what he could not say at that time. This is someone who in other verses in the Gospel of John is juxtaposed to another entity called the Comforter and is only described in one verse as the Holy Ghost, which was the King James translation. Newer translations such as the New Revised Standard Version translate it as Holy Spirit which would coincide with the Spirit of Truth concept.

In John 14:16-17 the term Comforter is first used in John. In this set of verses the Comforter and the Spirit of Truth are separate entities. Jesus described the Comforter as someone / something that will be with the community of believers forever. Obviously, this is not a Prophet because a Prophet is only with the community for a set time and then he passes on to the next world.

In John 14:25-26, the King James Version explicitly notes that the Comforter is the Holy Ghost or in later versions as noted above the Holy Spirit. As discussed earlier in this book, the Holy Ghost is known as *Ruh* in Islam. The *Ruh* is the Archangel Gabriel who brought messages from God to His Prophets. It would make sense that the Holy Ghost lives forever since he would be an angel in Islam, but in Christianity the Holy Ghost is the spirit of God which is considered a separate deity in the trinity. There are some issues with this theological perspective though. It is not clear in Christianity what the Holy Ghost actually is and if it is a separate deity how is it that Jesus will send it when it is already there. Remember, the Holy Ghost came upon Jesus after his Baptism in the Book of Matthew.

In Christianity, it is believed that people who are devout followers of Christ can also prophesize in his name. Remember the verse above regarding Jesus' refutation of those who do this. Paul thought that he was doing this. There have been many Christians throughout the ages that have come forward claiming to be prophesying in the name of Jesus, creating their own sects of Christianity, and a part of this tradition in Christianity is the belief that the Holy Ghost is communicating to them because Jesus supposedly said in these verses in the Bible that it would come to tell them what Jesus did not tell his disciples. The historical inconsistency between this tradition and the established religion of Christianity as embodied by the Catholic Church initially in Western Europe is that when people came forward with their own messages claiming to be receiving this guidance they were immediately deemed heretics and burned at the stake.[111] Apparently, only the Pope was granted this privilege.

There is no wonder given this interpretation of the teaching of Jesus regarding the Comforter that there are hundreds of sects of Christianity. This is not to say that Islam does not have a number of sects as well. The divisions in the Muslim community circulate around the person of the *Mahdi* who was prophesized to come before the coming of Jesus to lead the Muslim community. There have been many *Mahdis* in Islam such as the one that started the Bahai faith and the one that started the Ahmadiyah faith. The early sectarian split in Islam also involved Ali worship which has evolved into the modern-day sect known as the Shia (Party of Ali) which was an outgrowth of an early conflict between the companions of the Prophet after the third *Caliphate*. Ali was the fourth *Caliph* of Islam who was killed by a group known as the Kharijites whose modern-day descendants would be groups like al-Qaeda, non-state actors who thought they were the only ones following the true Islam and they were willing to kill anyone who seemingly opposed them. Ali was one of the first converts to Islam as discussed in the opening to Chapter 2.

The Comforter is mentioned several other times in John. In John 15:26-27 the dichotomy between the Comforter and the Spirit of Truth is made again. Even from the pure Christian perspective it is not easy to understand who the Comforter is as opposed to the Spirit of Truth. The Islamic perspective would identify the Spirit of Truth as a direct reference to the Prophet Muhammad. It can easily be interpreted from the Islamic perspective as well that the Comforter is a reference to the Prophet Muhammad, but it cannot be said with any certainty.

---

[111] Frassetto, M. (2010). *The Great Medieval Heretics: Five Centuries of Religious Dissent.* New York, NY: BlueBridge.

In John 16:7-8 the Comforter is mentioned again without any reference to the Spirit of Truth. In this set of verses Jesus stated that he must
leave so that the Comforter will come to the believers. Jesus stated in
verse 8 that the Comforter will clear the world of sin and spread righteousness and bring proper judgment. It is difficult to read these descriptions without thinking that the Comforter is a Prophet, because this is
what Prophets do in this world. The angels do not do this. The Holy
Ghost, an invisible entity in Christian teachings that is not clearly understood if it is conceptualized as something separate from the angels, also
does not do this. As stated earlier in this book in the section 'Sending of
Prophets' on pages 173–176 the angels and other unseen creatures were
not sent to people because mankind has nothing in common with them.
In Islam, Prophets are sent to their own people so that the message is
easier to digest. If an angel came with the various messages and spoke
to mankind they would be so enthralled with the angel itself that the
message would never pass into their hearts. Plus later generations will
say that it was merely a legend and discard the notion that an actual
angel came and brought the message to the people.

Lastly, it needs to be stated that Jesus in the Gospels never said that he
was the final Prophet. There are verses in the Gospels that highlight the
importance of Jesus at that time such as in John 14:6 where Jesus stated
that no one comes to the Father, i.e. God, except through him. At the time
Jesus was stating this to the disciples this makes sense because all Prophets
came and stated that they were bringing the truth that if people accept it
they will be saved and if they reject it they will be lost. This is not different in Islam. Still, making this claim to the disciples is not as sweeping as
saying to the disciples that he is the final Prophet and that all others after
him that claim a similar status are liars. This claim is explicitly made in the
Qur'an though in Chapter 33 verse 40 in which it is stated that Muhammad is the Messenger of God and the last of the Prophets. In some translations the 'last of the Prophets' is translated as 'seal of the Prophets'. One
of the names given to Muhammad in Islam is the 'Seal of the Prophets'.
As a matter of fact, none of the Prophets in the Old Testament or New
Testament made this claim. Only Muhammad made this claim.

CHAPTER 13

A REFUTATION OF COMMON CRITICISMS OF ISLAM

A Refutation of Common Criticisms of Islam

This chapter dedicates some space to addressing some of the common criticisms of Islam. As discussed earlier in this book, the purpose of this book is to refute the idea that Jesus and Muhammad taught dramatically different religions. Most of the books and articles on this topic attempt to define the differences to exacerbate a gap between Christians and Muslims. This has moved from simply an academic discussion to a policy-oriented one with proposals for Muslims in the United States subjected to 'religious tests' on their support for *sharia* (Islamic law), equality between men and women and disavowal of violence.[112]

This chapter addresses several issues. These include the assumptions that Islam promotes militancy and violence, the subjugation of women, the encouragement of lying and falsehood and the imposition of *sharia* on non-Muslims. This listing is not comprehensive, but some of the major issues that are discussed in some circles at the time of writing this chapter.

One common accusation is that the Prophet Muhammad was a war-monger who spread Islam from the tip of a sword. One cannot read the various characterizations of Muhammad and not walk away and think that he was the evilest man to ever have lived in this world and in extension anyone who practices Islam is evil. The best place to start in a rebuttal to these claims is with the reason for the first permission to go to war given to the nascent Muslim community who had

---

[112] Woodruff, B. (2016, November 21). Kobach Accidentally Reveals Anti-Muslim Plan - The Daily Beast. Retrieved from http://www.thedailybeast.com/articles/2016/11/21/kobach-accidentally-reveals-anti-muslim-plan.html

just migrated from Mecca to Medina. Besides the fact that the Meccans were slowly killing them off culminating in an assassination attempt on Muhammad himself, once the Muslims migrated to Medina the Meccans confiscated all their property in Mecca. This was a clear violation of one of the central rights of Islam which is the protection of life and property. It was within this context that the permission to fight was given to the migrating Muslims. As it states Chapter 22 verse 39 (the first verse that gave permission to fight), "To those against whom war is made, permission is given (to fight) because they are wronged, and verily, Allah is most powerful for their aid."[113]

In this verse it clearly states that fighting is permitted against those who fight against them. The claim that these verses were abrogated by later verses in the Qur'an is not supported by a consensus of the Islamic scholars. As discussed earlier in this book, abrogation is something real in Islam, but in Islamic scholarship one needs much knowledge and training even to state that something has been abrogated by something later in the Qur'an and even then it is a highly contentious discussion.

This core verse in the Qur'an regarding the permission to fight is supported in other verses revealed during the Medinan period. For example, in Chapter 2 verse 190 it states that the Muslims are only allowed to fight those that fight them and they are warned that they are not allowed to transgress the boundaries. Another verse on this issue states in Chapter 8 verse 61 that the Muslims are to incline towards peace if the enemy inclines towards it.

There are great examples of restraint such as the Treaty of Hudaybiyyah and more emphasis on peace such as the bloodless taking of Mecca after the Meccans broke the Treaty. This does not hide the fact that Muhammad was a warrior-prophet. He and his followers fought like the Israelite prophets fought, but they did so with great restraint and within the Laws of God. If one is going to criticize Muhammad for fighting for his faith then one should be prepared to criticize the

---

[113] Ali, A. Y. (2010). *The Meaning of the Glorious Qur'an*. Istanbul, Turkey: ASIR Media. (p. 225).

prophets of Israel. One should also be prepared to criticize the long history of crusades and inquisitions in the history of Christianity.

Some have also argued that the Prophet Muhammad did all of this for his own benefit, power and greed which is invalidated by the story of his life. Everything he gained, he gave away to the poor. There is an interesting exchange between one of his greatest companions, Umar, and Muhammad when Umar saw him sleeping on a mat on the floor and he cried, "O Allah's Messenger! Caesar (King of Byzantium) and Khosrau (King of Persia) are leading the life (i.e. luxurious life) while you, Allah's Messenger though you are, is living in destitute." The Prophet responded that, "Won't you be satisfied that they enjoy this world and we the Hereafter?"[114]

Another accusation made about Islam and its teachings is that it encourages its followers to lie and deceive others particularly non-Muslims. This is known as *taqiyyah*. According to Yarden Mariuma, a faculty member in the Department of Sociology at Columbia University, *taqiyyah* is the, "permission to dissimulate, and even deny one's faith in times of personal danger."[115]

The definition of *taqiyyah* has shifted over time with contradictory meanings. As noted by Mariuma, "taqiyya, as a concept, arose from survival mechanisms, became a spiritual discipline, and the meaning of the term is deeply embedded in the place and time in which it is used."[116] Further Mariuma notes that, "building on textual analysis and ethnography, then, polemicists use the concept of Taqiyya frequently to make certain claims about their own societies' ability to deal with "The Muslim threat". There are many specific meanings of the term: a polemicist can choose which he wishes to transfer to the present, leaving all others behind him, buried in unread journals and reli-

---

[114] Sahih Bukhari Vol. 6, Book 60, Hadith 435. This hadith can be read in its entirety here: http://sunnah.com/urn/45900.

[115] Mariuma, Y. (2014). Taqiyya as Polemic, Law and Knowledge: Following an Islamic Legal Term through the Worlds of Islamic Scholars, Ethnographers, Polemicists and Military Men. *The Muslim World, 104*(1-2), 91.

[116] Ibid. p. 97.

gious texts."[117] In addition Mariuma explains that, "as opposed to learned arguments among Muslim scholars, the non-Muslim writers who use Taqiyya as a form of Islamophobic polemic attack are actually quite crude, but struggle towards the same vision of convincing the reader that statements by Muslims about harmony and "fitting in" are false."[118]

In the Qur'an it states that the Muslims are not allowed to conceal the truth. In Chapter 2 verse 42 it explains quite clearly that the truth and falsehood are not equivalent and Muslims are not to conceal the truth. In addition, the Qur'an makes it clear that giving false testimony is a crime. In Chapter 25 verses 71 – 72 it states that the righteous are those that do not give false testimony. As Ibn Kathir explained regarding this verse the believers are not to bear witness to falsehood which includes lies, foul speech and false words. They do not do any of these things nor do they give audience to anyone engaged in this behavior.

Further, the Qur'an implores that Muslims do not speak about something they have no knowledge about i.e. giving potentially false information. In Chapter 17 verse 36 it states that the Muslims are not to follow those things in which they have no knowledge. In this verse the Muslims are commanded to not say anything of which they have no knowledge. Testifying to falsehood is one of those things that will be a problem for someone when they face judgment in the next life.

There were times in the early days of Islam and after when the Muslims were weak and oppressed. In certain circumstances they could renounce their faith out of fear. The renunciation of faith in Islam is something that is not taken lightly as it states in Chapter 16 verses 106 – 107 that anyone who renounces faith unless compelled will receive the wrath of God.

In these verses it is made clear that apostasy is something not liked by God however in times when the Muslims are compelled, they can renounce it while keeping the faith in the heart. This is the possible reason for Peter's denial of Jesus in John 18. According to the Book

---

[117] Ibid. p. 97.

[118] Ibid. p. 98 – 99.

of John, Jesus is said to have said to Peter that he would deny him three times before the cock crows. Christians revere Peter as one of the greatest disciples of Jesus yet when Palestine was aflame with hatred towards Jesus and his followers Peter, in fear for his life, lied about his affiliation with Jesus.

The other side of the issue is the worry among some that Muslims deliberately lie as a strategy of warfare. This concept does not come from the Qur'an, but the *hadith* in which it states in Sahih Bukhari that war is deception.[119] In this frame, Muslims will use any means necessary to win a war including deceiving the enemy by lying to them through *taqiyyah*. Of course, name a war where one did not attempt to deceive its enemy. The ancient Greeks were said to have used the Trojan horse to defeat Troy and in the Bible Gideon's defeat of the Midianites involved deception in Judges 7. Still, it would be highly fallacious to assume that Muslim Americans are at war with the United States and therefore their neighbors.

Another accusation about Islam is that it teaches its followers to hate Jews. It is often assumed that Muslims hate Jews and Jews hate Muslims. The Muslims did not have contact with the Jewish tribes of Medina until the migration from Mecca to Medina thirteen years after the first revelation. When Muhammad arrived he initiated a covenant with the people of Medina including the Jewish tribes there. This has been known throughout the ages as the 'Constitution of Medina'. Through this constitution the concept of the *ummah* was established on the basis of a security pact between the Muslims, pagans and Jews who lived in Medina.

In article 15 of this constitution it states that the Jews are part of the *ummah* along with all others that joined the covenant. It is recognized in this article that the Jews have their religion and the Muslims have their own religion. This is a specific nod to the Jewish community in Medina which was already addressed in general in Chapter 109. Muslims cannot impose their religion on other people nor can others impose their religion on them.[120]

---

[119] Chapter 73, #1298

[120] Arjomand, S. A. (2009). The Constitution of Medina: A Socio-legal Interpretation of Muhammad's Acts of Foundation of the Umma. *International Journal of Middle*

As noted by Arjomand, "the lasting effect of the constitutional recognition of the Jews' religion was the institution of religious pluralism
in Islam. Muhammad's constitutional settlement concerning the Jewish clans of Medina, by contrast, did not have any lasting effect."[121]
The first Jewish tribe to rebel and thereby break this agreement was
the Bani Qaynuqa. This was followed by two more Jewish tribes. The
first two were banished after breaking the agreement and the final one
was punished in line with Deuteronomy 20:10 – 17.

This was the last major incident of Muslim and Jewish violence.
One more problem erupted in Khaybar, where many of the exiled Jewish tribesmen had fled from Medina. After these fortresses fell, the
Jewish tribes were pacified and were allowed to remain on their land
in exchange for a rent.

The Muslims and Jews never had problems after this until the present-day with the issue in Palestine. Quite the contrary, the Jews helped
the Muslims wrestle territory away from the Romans and other Christian groups because the Christians had treated them so poorly. For
example, when the Muslims defeated the Visigoths at the capital of
Cordoba in present-day Spain the Jews were actually put in charge of
the city.

It is very likely that if there was not a contention over Palestine, the
Muslims and Jews would be as close today as they were in history. For
example, Albania, a predominantly Muslim country in Europe, saved
the Jews they could from European fascism and possible extermination
during World War 2. A documentary titled 'Besa: The Promise' was
made about this.[122]

In a related issue, many have made negative associations with *sharia*. The spread of anti-*sharia* laws across the United States indicates
that this negative association has materialized into a tangible threat for
lawmakers and their constituents. This idea proliferates even though
knowledge about *sharia* is extraordinarily limited in the United States.

East Studies, 41(04), 555-575.

[121] Ibid. p. 561.

[122] Information on the documentary can be found at this website: http://besath-epromise.com/.

Sharia is Islamic Law. Everything from financial law, family law and criminal law are all subsumed under this title as well as the mundane practices of Muslims from day to day. Muslims believe that faith and law are joined together much like believers in Judaism. *Sharia* is for Muslims only.

History has shown that Muslim rulers did not impose *sharia* upon their non-Muslim subjects. According to Stefanos Katsikas, the Ottoman Empire instituted a 'millet' system. A millet is a Turkish term for 'people' or 'nation'. The Christians and Jews of the Empire enjoyed a special status in which they were organized into self-governing religious communities. Each millet was headed the religious leader of the group which was based in the capital, Istanbul. This official had responsibilities beyond religious including, "a number of civil areas, such as education, the management of millet properties and the administration of justice in cases related to canon law, such as debt, divorce, adoption and inheritance, through the appointment of ecclesiastical courts to deal with these."[123]

This system implies that these communities managed their own affairs in which the laws binding to Muslims i.e. the *sharia* were not imposed on the non-Muslim communities of the Empire. The idea that Muslims are trying to impose Islamic Law on non-Muslims in Europe or the United States is ludicrous which has no historical precedent. The anti-*sharia* movement in the United States and elsewhere is baseless and rooted more in fear-mongering towards the Muslim community.

Lastly, one of the major accusations about Islam is that it is oppressive towards women. This is repeated frequently in books, online and on television. There is mixed evidence of this accusation, but there are clear indications in Islam that women are more respected than is typically given credit.

A *hadith* is reported in Sahih Bukhari which states that when asked about who is the most deserving of good companionship, the Prophet responded that it is one's mother. He repeated this several times to

---

[123] Katsikas, S. (2009). Millets in Nation-States: The Case of Greek and Bulgarian Muslims, 1912–1923. *Nationalities Papers*, *37*(2), 178.

reinforce the point and then he said one's father after this.[124] This has been covered in this book already. In Islam as in Christianity respect for one's parents is paramount. In this *hadith*, the emphasis is placed on the mother. How can a religion which places so much respect on the mother hate women?

In another *hadith*, the Prophet warned the Muslims that there are several things that are forbidden for them. This included being undutiful to one's mother. In addition, the Prophet mentioned the killing of daughters which was a pagan Arab practice before Islam. These two points emphasize the high value of women in Islam which dramatically changed Arab culture at the time.[125]

Further, the Prophet Muhammad told the Muslims that the best of them were those that were best to their families.[126] It is difficult to read this *hadith* and not understand the importance of the family in Islam. The mother not only has a high status, but Muslim men are told that if they wish to be counted amongst the best people they are to treat their wife and children in the best way.

M. Steven Fish, a professor in comparative politics at UC Berkeley, in his great book on the Muslim world "Are Muslims Distinctive: A Look at the Evidence" explored the place of women in the Islamic world today.[127] In general, he found when exploring attitudes towards gender inequality and actual gender inequality represented by life expectancy and literacy that women fair poorly in the Islamic world however he did find that gender differences had a larger role to play than religious differences between Muslim and non-Muslim populations.

Fish avoided blaming Islam for this discrepancy. He wrote, "Al-Bukhari's reports are replete with passages that depict women as leaders and spiritual counselors...."[128] Fish elaborated that, "In al-Bukhari's depiction of the Prophet's community, rigorous segregation of the

---

[124] Book 8, Vol. 73, # 2

[125] Sahih Bukhari, Book 43, # 23

[126] Reported in Sunan At-Tirmidhi # 3895

[127] Fish, M. S. (2011). *Are Muslims distinctive?: A look at the evidence*. Oxford, U.K.: Oxford University Press.

[128] Ibid. p. 207.

sexes in daily life, reflexive female subordination to male authority, and sexual puritanism are simply absent."[129]

These observations indicate that the Prophet Muhammad and his early community in Medina treated women equally or at least more equally than they are treated in today's Islamic world. Fish further explained in his book possible reasons for this including the development of jurisprudence in the Islamic world informed more by the time than by the Qur'an or the traditions of the Prophet and the continual strength of tribalism in the Islamic world today.

The idea that women enjoyed a higher status under the Prophet Muhammad has been explored by a number of historians on the Islamic world. One of these historians is David Levering-Lewis, professor of history at New York University. In his book "God's Crucible: Islam and the Making of Europe, 570 – 1215" he explored the Great Fitna which was the great divide that occurred during the time of Ali's disputed Caliphate which led to the major schism in Islam (Sunni / Shia).[130] Ali was the first male convert to Islam and the husband to the Prophet's favorite daughter Fatima. He is considered one of the four Rightly-Guided Caliphs to follow after the death of the Prophet.

It is believed that Aisha, one of the Prophet's wives, did not like Ali very much and led a campaign against him in 656 AD. She is referred to by Sunni Muslims as 'Mother of the Believers' because a large portion of the knowledge of the Prophet is derived from her accounts. Those that rode against Ali did not believe he had the right to rule the Islamic world. In the end, Ali and his forces were victorious and Aisha was captured, pardoned by Ali and put under house arrest in Medina.

It is at this point that Levering-Lewis described the beginning of the subjugation of women in the Islamic world by stating that, "Not only did it open the Pandora's box of civil war but it would encourage Muslim men to justify the exclusion thereafter of Muslim women from participation in public life. Muhammad's comparatively enlightened ideas (as explained by Allah) about gender roles positively distinguished the Qur'an from its misogynistic Mosaic and Pauline ana-

---

[129] Ibid. p. 208.

[130] Lewis, D. L. (2008). *God's crucible: Islam and the making of Europe, 570 to 1215.* New York, NY: W. W. Norton.

logues. In the last analysis, though, scripture is no better than the society through which it lives, and the Prophet's ideas about women's rights cut across the patriarchal grain of his race, place and time. Muslim women had fought side by side with their men in the early battles, their ululations and fierceness often striking fear in the enemy and carrying the day. The Khadijas, Hinds, Hafsas, and other women of ability and initiative continued to exert a presence in the affairs of the ummah, but they would gradually be pressed under the weight of the traditions and institutions interpreted and constructed by men for whom honor and war were paramount values."[131]

In these assessments by a well-respected social scientist and historian Muslim women in the early days of Islam and based on the traditions of the Prophet Muhammad and the Qur'an had much more equality and a better status than they enjoy today in the Islamic world. Many Muslims are coming to this realization and the role of women is starting to increase in the Islamic world. A classic book on this subject by Aisha Bewley discusses how Islam actually empowers women.[132] Some Muslim countries have had women presidents and women are starting to demand more from their governments, communities, families and people throughout the Islamic world.

In conclusion, the picture of Islam that is typically presented is rather limited and represent extreme bias. This book offers a counter-perspective with an emphasis on those things that Jesus and Muhammad have in common. This chapter has focused on refuting some claims made about Islam. It is argued that interpretations of warfare and women in Islam, for example, lack the appropriate insight into the actual teachings of Islam. These accusations are the center-piece of most of the criticisms of Islam which has almost become a mantra. Islam is violent and oppresses women. This chapter has shown that this belief is not solid.

---

[131] Ibid. p. 89 – 90.

[132] Bewley, A. A. (1999). *Islam: The empowering of women* (2nd ed.). London, U.K.: Ta-Ha.

CHAPTER 14

CONCLUSIONS

Conclusions

This book is focused on the Prophetic teachings of Jesus and Muhammad and how they are similar and different. The contexts are narrowed as much as possible to make this comparison as valid as possible. Most of the chapters in this book only include verses in the Qur'an that were revealed in the Meccan period except Chapters 10 and 11 which highlight the contradictions and similarities between the teachings in the Gospels and the teachings in the Qur'an, respectively. In fact, there are more verses in the Gospels that have counterparts in the Qur'an than there are contradictions.

The first part of this book focuses on the first three years of the revelation of the Qur'an when the Prophet Muhammad and the few early believers were practicing what they knew of Islam at that time in secret. This time period of revelation also matches the time that Jesus is believed to have preached in Palestine. It was found in Chapter 3 that practically all of the teachings of Muhammad in this period are comparable to the teachings of Jesus.

The second part of this book expands the Qur'anic revelations beyond the first three years to include the last ten years in Mecca. During this time period the condition of the believers in Mecca matched the conditions of the believers in Palestine during the time of Jesus. In both circumstances Muhammad and Jesus and their followers were being oppressed by a dominant group. In Palestine it was the Pharisees and in Mecca it was the Quraysh in which both of these groups conspired to kill them.

In both the Gospels and the Qur'an there are many verses with similar messages regarding disbelief which was covered in Chapter 5. In Chapter 6 the commands given to the believers in the Gospels and the Qur'an are compared in which both enjoin their followers to forgive and be patient. In addition in this chapter there are many beliefs and behaviors that are emphasized such as believing in personal responsibility for their own actions, being respectful of one's parents, not being arrogant, avoiding sexual deviations and greeting each other in peace.

The rewards of God given to mankind is a topic covered in both the Qur'an and the Gospels as covered in Chapter 7. In both books this life is considered transitory while the next life is considered the real life worth striving for with good deeds and faith. One of the means of achieving the good end in the hereafter is to give charity which is emphasized in both the Qur'an and the Gospels.

The story of Jesus is explored in Chapter 8 in which the beginning of the story in the Book of Luke and in Chapter Maryam in the Qur'an are the only comparable elements of the stories in the two messages. The Gospels do not contain any stories of former Prophets while the Qur'an has a number of these stories ranging from other Prophets to wise men. Both the Qur'an and the Gospels also have parables that are very similar to each other such as the parables regarding the good soil and weak foundations.

In Chapter 9 both the Qur'an and the Gospels have many comparable messages on explanations related to faith and the realities of life on earth and in the hereafter. They explain the reason for the Prophets being sent to mankind and how they were subservient to God. They explain how the Words of God cannot change and that those who are only focused on this life eventually end up losing their real life which is in the hereafter. In both messages God is described as All-Knowing while in the Qur'an and the Gospels there are various prophecies that had either come true after the fact or have not come true as of yet.

The contradictions between the messages in the Gospels and the Qur'an are highlighted in Chapter 10 in which these contradictions involve marriage, divorce, Jesus dying, fasting while the Prophets are amongst them, the hereafter state of man, the forgiveness of sins through the death of Jesus and the declaration that Jesus is the Son of God. In this chapter it is further explored on why these contradictions exist such as through different contexts or translation/transmission/alteration issues.

Chapter 11 provides a counter to these contradictions in which a number of verses found in Medina that agree with the Gospels are covered in detail. Both messages state that the Prophets are servants of God, those who believe must love the Prophets above all, the powers of Jesus are true, the Prophets are judges, the Prophets brought new messages, believers should not show off when fasting, leadership should be servitude, there should be the testimony of two men for contracts and the exhortation to migrate from a place of oppression. These similarities emphasize that not only during the Meccan period, but including the Medinan period the messages in the Qur'an and the Gospels have more similarities than differences.

Chapter 12 points out some controversial teachings that can be found in the Gospels such as the use of the sword, sentiments towards non-believers and beliefs about opponents. These controversial teachings much like those that many uncover in the Qur'an are not numerous, but require further explanation to fully understand their meaning. Similar to those supposedly controversial teachings in the Qur'an there are multiple explanations for their meanings.

Finally, chapter 13 explores the possibility that Muhammad is mentioned in the Gospels. In particular, the Gospel of John provides many references to two seemingly separate entities, the 'Spirit of Truth' and the 'Comforter'. Since Jesus is reported to have said that his message was incomplete, it leaves open the possibility that these references are to the Prophet Muhammad.

Epilogue

This book has been an effort to bridge a gap between Christians and Muslims that has existed since the first migrants of the Muslim community appeared in Ethiopia and the generals of the Negus grumbled about the beliefs of the Muslims regarding Jesus. The Prophet Muhammad also sent a letter while in Medina to the Christian Caesar of Byzantium declaring his Prophethood in which the Caesar showed interest while his generals rejected it. In addition, Abu Amir was a Christian monk who had lived in Medina before the arrival of Muhammad, but after his arrival left Medina to agitate against him including building a controversial mosque in Quba. Lastly, before the passing of Muhammad the Muslims had to mobilize against the Byzantines who were threatening invasion. The rest is history culminating in the Muslim invasion of Jerusalem, Constantinople and Spain while the Christians engaged in seven Crusades and the Inquisition in Spain which encompassed the first, but not the last, genocide of Muslims in Europe.

I feel that there is more the Christians and Muslims can do together in understanding each other in mutual respect than in allowing hatred to spread towards each other which in history has never ended well for either community. In the 1990s there was the Muslim Bosnian genocide and in 2014 the genocide of Muslims in the Central African Republic by Christians. In Iraq and Egypt following the collapse of their governments the attack on Christians who had lived there peacefully alongside Muslims for centuries is a disturbing development. It is depressing to think that these recent deadly developments are setting the tone for the 21st Century.

This book is thoroughly couched in the Muslim perspective regarding the messages of Jesus so there are many objections that Christians may have regarding the interpretations included in here. The point of this book is not to erase fundamental differences between Muslims and Christians, but to provide an exegesis on how most of the teachings found in the Gospels can also be found in the Qur'an. The conclusion that one can take from this is that the Muslims have more in common with Christians than they have differences. This should facilitate more cooperation between the two faith groups than discord.

The secondary revelation of this text is how it is very possible that Jesus and Muhammad were both communicating the Words of God. On the part of Christians this would require recognizing Muhammad as a Prophet of God which would fundamentally change their view of their own faith. For me this meant conversion to Islam, but for others it could have a different impact.

It is hoped with this project that at the very least Muslims and Christians can understand each other better and engage in a lasting dialogue over the religions of Christianity and Islam. In the end, a peaceful and civil discussion over the issues covered in this book such as the contradictions between Islam and Christianity is all that can be asked for in this life. Many are pushing in the opposite direction attempting to agitate for conflict and hatred which is counter-productive and destructive. The missionary zeal of both Muslims and Christians needs to have limits on how disrespectful each community is in communicating its message. Christians who say abhorrent things about Muhammad and the Qur'an are doing more consequently to lead to oppressions towards Christians in the Muslim world. The production of a repulsive video about Muhammad by a Coptic Christian hurt the Coptic community in Egypt who existed even before the Muslims arrived in Egypt. The burning of the Qur'an by an evangelical Christian in north Florida only increased hatred towards Christians in the Muslim world. The actions of the Islamic State in Iraq and Syria (ISIS) have done similar things regarding the hatred of Christians towards Muslims. Peace and respect is the plea in this book.

Index